Writing Lessons for the Overhead

Grades 5 and Up

by Lola M. Schaefer

SCHOLASTIC
PROFESSIONAL BOOKS

NEW YORK ● TORONTO ● LONDON ● AUCKLAND ● SYDNEY
MEXICO CITY ● NEW DELHI ● HONG KONG ● BUENOS AIRES

For the dedicated teachers of student writers—
keep demonstrating and encouraging

Acknowledgments

Thank you, Connie, for continuing as my classroom mentor.

Again, my sincere appreciation to my editor Joanna Davis-Swing,
who wants the very best for classroom teachers.

Excerpt from *Hope Was Here* by Joan Bauer. Copyright © 2000 by Joan Bauer. Used by permission of
G.P. Putnam's Sons, an imprint of Penguin Putnam Books for Young Readers, a division of Penguin
Putnam Inc. All rights reserved.

Cover design by James Sarfati
Interior design by Sarah Morrow

5 6 7 8 9 10   40   09 08 07 06 05 04

Contents

Introduction

Mini-Lessons That Ignite Thoughtful Writing

Teaching writing is not an easy task. It requires knowledge, organization, conferencing skills, classroom management skills, and practice. In addition, it calls for a sensibility to the strengths and weaknesses of each writer and an appreciation for the truly personal commitment he or she makes when putting pen to paper. For all these reasons and more, teachers of writing are constantly seeking new tools to help them guide students through the writing process.

Mini-lessons are essential components of any classroom writing model. By design, they are 5–12 minute whole or small group learning opportunities in which the teacher, or another writer, introduces or revisits a practice for future use. Mini-lessons can provide instruction or strategies for following procedures, mining an idea, determining purpose and form, choosing the elements of craft, creating titles, revising, editing, or publishing work. But as I travel to schools and demonstrate the writing process, it appears that teachers are most concerned with how to help their students improve the quality of their writing. They are searching for mini-lessons that will help students strengthen their writing.

For the past six years, I have been visiting K–8 classrooms, directly helping students work through the writing cycle. Because of my limited demonstration time, I must make the most of my mini-lessons. To this end, I composed groups of writing samples that serve as models of how writers use craft elements. These pieces are not meant to be perfect examples of writing, but rather meaningful illustrations that are especially designed for middle-school students by content, length, style, and tone. These pieces launch students into discussion and discovery of what works in strong writing—and what doesn't, since each set of examples includes weak writing as well as strong. Each set of samples focuses on one craft element. Many of these same craft elements are the criteria used to evaluate content and form on state standardized tests.

When I present mini-lessons on craft elements, I place the two to four models on the overhead projector and read each with enthusiasm and expression. Never stating my opinion, I ask the students to critically examine these short samples together. Through a series of questions, I guide students to state what they think the author did well and what could be improved. They are pleased to assume the role of evaluator. Often students decide quickly which is the strongest sample and support their decisions with specific references to the text. The unexpected carryover is that their next drafts reflect their observations and assessments. Students become even more thoughtful writers, incorporating some of these craft elements into their pieces.

Currently, many intermediate teachers not only teach their own content curriculum, but also integrate more reading and writing into their subject areas. Some of these teachers struggle to find supplemental materials that can help them guide their students in the craft of clean, succinct writing. With time constraints always a defining issue, they, too, are looking for mini-lessons to help their students zero in on key writing elements. The examples in this book could be one resource for these teachers as well as language arts and reading teachers.

Mini-lessons are not quick fixes. They are seeds that rest in fertile minds until they sprout and grow within a meaningful context. Take the time to talk with your students, writer to writer. Let them learn with you through your questions and experimentation. Offer brief, daily mini-lessons to provide your students with the additional tools they need to cultivate a love of writing now and always. The mini-lessons and writing models in this book are resources you can return to throughout the year as you and your students grow together as writers.

How to Use the Samples in This Book

The writing models and lessons in this book are not intended to replace discussions centered around published writing, peer critiques, or teacher conferences. Instead, they are a supplement to be used to enhance understanding of specific craft elements—an understanding that will then strengthen student writing. Each mini-lesson focuses on a writing skill and provides teaching strategies for using models related to this skill. You can use a set of samples within a mini-lesson when you observe that your students need more specific help in learning one particular element of writing. You can use them to:

1. introduce a new craft element to your students.
2. reinforce efforts you've seen your students make.
3. review one particular element before some students engage in peer critique.
4. nudge students into revision with a specific element in mind.

I have had the greatest results when reusing the same samples within a short time frame. For instance, if I'm working with sixth graders on paragraph organization, I might introduce the organization of topic sentence, supporting details, and conclusion with one set, and guide students to discover which sample or samples have the strongest organization. A few days later, when some students are moving into peer critiques and revision, I'll place those same examples, or another set, on the overhead projector. I'll lead them through a discussion so they can again identify the structure that helps organize a piece of writing. With students emotionally involved in their own pieces, they are more likely to re-examine their writing with a critical eye to find opportunities where they can improve organization.

The anonymity of the pieces ensures a safe, comfortable environment for discussion. Many middle-school students worry about what their peers think, so using the samples from this text will provide them with a sense of comfort. They won't have to worry that their writing, named or anonymous, will suddenly appear on the overhead projector. These samples are simply working models, with no personal consequences of fame or shame for anyone in the classroom.

I recommend using one set of samples for at least two weeks before introducing another craft element. We want intermediate students to identify, apply, practice, and recognize each writing element before adding another; revisiting the same element with the same samples builds their awareness and reinforces their understanding of a particular craft element. After you see the power of these kinds of pieces, you may want to generate additional examples for your students.

We teach the tools of writing so students will be able to communicate more effectively. Our main goal, always, is to provide the strategies and skills that enable every student to express his or her thoughts and ideas. Use these samples to enhance your students' understanding of the craft of writing. Then step back and encourage them to take risks and write boldly about what they know and feel.

Focus

Does All of the Writing Remain on One Topic?

A strong piece of writing focuses on one topic, providing appropriate development and details to support the topic. Focused writers know their purpose, audience, and content for a specific piece. Quite often writers list these intentions on a simple plan that they create during prewriting; a plan helps writers remain focused by giving them a point of reference during the writing process. If an author knows in advance what he or she wants to say and to whom, it is much easier to maintain the focus in a personal narrative, poem, fictional story, or informational essay.

Introducing the Craft Element: Focus

Begin your mini-lesson on focus like this:

Teacher: What do you do when you concentrate?

Student: I think hard about one thing. Like when I'm reading my science book, I think real hard about the words and nothing else.

Student: I try to keep other stuff from distracting me. Like at a soccer game, I concentrate on my feet dribbling the ball toward the goal. If the other team's players are yelling, I try to ignore what they're saying and just think about my feet and the ball.

Teacher: Great examples of concentration! Writers concentrate—or focus—on what they are writing. They try to keep all of their writing on one topic. They do not want unnecessary information or details to distract the reader from what they are trying to say. Let's look at three written samples and discover which one is most focused and why.

Discussing the Craft Element: Focus

Place sample #1 (page 11) of the *Focus* transparencies on the overhead projector. Read it out loud with expression. Afterward, ask these questions:

- Do you understand what the author has written?
- Does it make sense?

I always begin with these questions, for every sample we discuss. If the listener or reader doesn't understand the writing, it is pointless to continue. The purpose of this set of transparencies is to decide which piece is most focused and why. If the content or writing is confusing to the students, it will be difficult for them to discuss the issue of focus. As soon as you know that all students understand the piece, continue with these questions:

- What topic or subject has the author written about? (Encourage students to refer to the title and the first sentence to identify the topic.)
- Does all of the writing remain on that topic?
- Are there any phrases or sentences that lose that focus?
- Are there any words that need to be removed from this piece to improve the focus?

If students seem to miss obvious errors in focus, you may decide to read the piece again, one sentence at a time. After each sentence, ask if the information pertains to the topic they have stated. When students identify unnecessary language that takes the piece away from the focus, have one student use a bright color to highlight the words, phrases, or sentences that need to be deleted. Visual learners will respond well to this exercise. It is also a strategy that they can use with their own pieces when they are revising for focus.

Repeat this process for the other two examples in this set (page 12).

After you have read and discussed each sample, ask the students:
- Which piece is the most focused?
- What did this author do that made this writing more focused than the other two?

Discussion Points

If students cannot tell you why sample #2 is the most focused paragraph, ask these questions while showing that sample on the overhead projector:

- What is the author's topic or subject for this paragraph?
- When did we first know that this was the author's topic?
- What different aspects of his jitters does the author explain?
- Does every sentence have something to do with those few moments before he plays his recital pieces?

Clarify Focus: An Overview of the Craft Element

1. The title and first sentence give clues to the focus. The samples are titled "Piano Recital Jitters"; all three are about the author's nervousness at his piano recital.

2. Each sentence relates to the focus stated in the opening phrase: **As I nervously wait on stage with the other recital students.** The author describes what he does and how he feels while he waits for his turn: **looking out over the audience, sweaty hands, my fingers play Chopin's Etude;** his worries; how he tries to calm himself with encouraging thoughts; and finally how he begins his recital piece.

TIPS FOR WRITERS

What Can You Do to Remain Focused?

1. Identify the topic, audience, and purpose of the writing.
2. Create a brief plan before writing.
3. Reread each sentence and ask, "Does this writing remain on one topic?"
4. Ask a friend to read your draft and ask, "Do all of my sentences stay on the topic?"
5. Ask a friend to circle any words or phrases that are unnecessary and might take the piece away from the focus. Decide if you agree with your friend and remove any parts of your writing that are off of the focus.
6. Review your writing plan, and check to see if what you've written fulfills the purpose you had in mind when you began. Revise your composition if it has lost focus.

Piano Recital Jitters

As I nervously wait on stage with the other recital students, my fingers play Chopin's Etude on the sides of my legs. I look out over the faces in the audience. I see my neighbor Mrs. Schwartz. She attends all my piano recitals and soccer games. She says that I'm the grandson she never had. Mom and Dad are sitting next to her. They probably drove back home to get her after they dropped me off. My hands sweat, so I wipe my palms against my pants. Relax, I tell myself, but my heart races and my palms are wet again. I try to listen to the others, but instead I worry. *What if my hands shake so hard that I won't be able to play? What if I forget the notes and sit there like a statue at the keyboard? What if . . .* Applause interrupts my thoughts. It's my turn. I stand, wipe my hands once more, and walk to the bench. I sit and pull myself to the piano. It smells like furniture polish. Without hesitation my fingers find the keys. They know the notes and I know the music. Together we take command and the piano sings.

The highlighted sentences are off the focus of this piece

Piano Recital Jitters

As I nervously wait on stage with the other recital students, my fingers play Chopin's Etude on the sides of my legs. I look out over the faces in the audience. They intently watch Zach as his hands glide across the piano keys from one arpeggio to another. My hands sweat, so I wipe my palms against my pants. Relax, I tell myself. I know my Chopin and Mendelssohn by heart. I've been practicing them for more than two months. But my heart races and my palms are wet again. It's the waiting. I hate waiting. I try to listen to the others, but instead I worry. *What if my hands shake so hard that I won't be able to play? What if I forget the notes and sit there like a statue at the keyboard? What if . . .* Applause interrupts my thoughts. It's my turn. I stand, wipe my hands once more, and walk to the bench. I sit and pull myself to the piano. Without hesitation my fingers find the keys. They know the notes and I know the music. Together we take command and the piano sings.

All sentences relate to the focus of this piece.

Piano Recital Jitters

As I nervously wait on stage with the other recital students, my fingers play Chopin's Etude on the sides of my legs. I look out over the faces in the audience. They intently watch Zach as his hands glide across the piano keys from one arpeggio to another. He's a natural. With only one year of lessons, he plays better than most of us who began six years ago. I wipe my sweaty palms against my pants. Relax, I tell myself. But my heart races and my palms are wet again. It's the waiting. I hate waiting. I try to listen to the others, but instead I worry, like the time I was in line for the rollercoaster with my cousin. I worried so much that by the time it was our turn, I was too scared to get on. Uh-oh. It's my turn to play. I stand, wipe my hands once more, and walk to the bench. I sit and pull myself to the piano. My fingers know the notes and I know the music. Together we take command and the piano sings.

The highlighted sentences are off the focus of this piece.

Piano Recital Jitters 1

As I nervously wait on stage with the other recital students, my fingers play Chopin's Etude on the sides of my legs. I look out over the faces in the audience. I see my neighbor Mrs. Schwartz. She attends all my piano recitals and soccer games. She says that I'm the grandson she never had. Mom and Dad are sitting next to her. They probably drove back home to get her after they dropped me off. My hands sweat, so I wipe my palms against my pants. Relax, I tell myself, but my heart races and my palms are wet again. I try to listen to the others, but instead I worry. *What if my hands shake so hard that I won't be able to play? What if I forget the notes and sit there like a statue at the keyboard? What if* . . . Applause interrupts my thoughts. It's my turn. I stand, wipe my hands once more, and walk to the bench. I sit and pull myself to the piano. It smells like furniture polish. Without hesitation my fingers find the keys. They know the notes and I know the music. Together we take command and the piano sings.

Piano Recital Jitters 2

As I nervously wait on stage with the other recital students, my fingers play Chopin's Etude on the sides of my legs. I look out over the faces in the audience. They intently watch Zach as his hands glide across the piano keys from one arpeggio to another. My hands sweat, so I wipe my palms against my pants. Relax, I tell myself. I know my Chopin and Mendelssohn by heart. I've been practicing them for more than two months. But my heart races and my palms are wet again. It's the waiting. I hate waiting. I try to listen to the others, but instead I worry. *What if my hands shake so hard that I won't be able to play? What if I forget the notes and sit there like a statue at the keyboard? What if . . .* Applause interrupts my thoughts. It's my turn. I stand, wipe my hands once more, and walk to the bench. I sit and pull myself to the piano. Without hesitation my fingers find the keys. They know the notes and I know the music. Together we take command and the piano sings.

Piano Recital Jitters 3

As I nervously wait on stage with the other recital students, my fingers play Chopin's Etude on the sides of my legs. I look out over the faces in the audience. They intently watch Zach as his hands glide across the piano keys from one arpeggio to another. He's a natural. With only one year of lessons, he plays better than most of us who began six years ago. I wipe my sweaty palms against my pants. Relax, I tell myself. But my heart races and my palms are wet again. It's the waiting. I hate wait-ing. I try to listen to the others, but instead I worry, like the time I was in line for the roller coaster with my cousin. I worried so much that by the time it was our turn, I was too scared to get on. Uh-oh. It's my turn to play. I stand, wipe my hands once more, and walk to the bench. I sit and pull myself to the piano. My fingers know the notes and I know the music. Together we take command and the piano sings.

Vocabulary

THE QUESTION TO EXPLORE

Which Words Paint a Specific Picture?

Specific vocabulary helps a writer articulate exactly what he or she wants to communicate. I always tell students that writers are wordsmiths. Just as a blacksmith understands metals and knows how to shape them into works of art, a wordsmith understands words and can link them together to create artful images that evoke emotion in a reader. But unfortunately, many students today think, speak, and write with a limited vocabulary of only a few hundred words. The good news is that most students are eager to expand their working vocabularies, adding words that can precisely describe, explain, and inform. Once they are guided to an awareness of the power of specific language, they enjoy finding new words in the books they read and the conversations they hear in the classroom. They notice the difference in meaning and interest when exact vocabulary is used correctly. And they generously help one another improve the quality of their word choices during peer conferences and critiques.

Introducing the Craft Element: Vocabulary

Begin your mini-lesson on vocabulary like this:

Teacher: Listen and tell me what you see in your mind when I say the word *vehicle*.

Answers will vary from *minivan* to *train* to *airplane* to *ship* to *tractor trailer*.

Teacher: Now tell me what you see in your mind when I say *sailboat*.

Most answers will specifically describe the shape of the bow and sails of a sailboat.

Teacher: Which vocabulary was more specific? Which term painted a more detailed picture in your mind? *Vehicle?* Or *sailboat?*

If you want to extend this exercise, other examples of words you might offer the students are: *floor* and *basketball court*; *liked* and *cherished*; *patterned* and *crisscrossed*; *moved* and *lunged*; *bit* and *nibbled*; *took* and *confiscated*; and *award* and *medallion*.

The purpose of this short exercise is to help students discover that precise vocabulary provides the reader/listener with a specific image. The more exact the vocabulary, the better the writer can communicate what he or she is thinking. Specific vocabulary adds detail—the substance of description and explanation—making the piece more interesting to readers.

Follow-up

You can reinforce the importance of specific vocabulary with this activity. Let students compare the meaning and interest of two sentences on the same topic. One is written with general, or vague, vocabulary, the other with precise word choice.

Teacher: Please, listen to this sentence:
The dancer tripped on something and fell.
Now, tell me what you saw in your head when I said that sentence.

Give several students an opportunity to describe what they saw in their minds when they heard the sentence. While they are reporting, ask them questions: *What kind of dancer did you envision? Was it a male or female? What did that person trip on? How did he or she fall?* Count how many different images that this one sentence created in the minds of the students.

Teacher: Now listen to this sentence:
The ballerina tripped on the stage curtain and stumbled head-first into her partner.

Again, ask a few students to describe what they saw in their minds as you said this sentence.

Teacher: Which of these sentences provides the most exact picture in your mind? Which words are more specific? *Ballerina* or *dancer*? *Something* or *stage curtain*? *Stumbled* or *fell*? An author wants to choose words that offer his or her audience the most precise picture.

Put Some Meat on Those Bones

❋

Students enjoy revising a bare bone sentence written with general language into a meaty image with specific vocabulary. After modeling with the dancer/ballerina sentence, you can offer your students one of the following sentences to rewrite with precise word choice. Suggest that students brainstorm a short list of word choices for nouns and verbs before writing their revision.

> *The dog walked after the boy.*
>
> *The student worked hard at her desk.*
>
> *Many stars were in the sky.*
>
> *It tasted good to him.*
>
> *The tree was tall.*
>
> *The child played on the floor.*
>
> *The ground was wet and soft under his feet.*
>
> *The car went really fast.*

I recommend doing only one sentence at a time to keep the exercise fresh. Also, students will want to hear what other students wrote, so allow time for this exchange. I usually have students share their revision in groups of three and then select one person from each group to share with the whole class.

This short exercise gives students excellent practice in identifying imprecise language and replacing it with words and phrases that are vivid and exact.

Discussing the Craft Element: Vocabulary

Place Set A of the *Vocabulary* transparencies (page 19) on the overhead projector. Read sample #1 out loud to the students with expression. Ask these questions:

- Do you understand what the author has written? Does it make sense?

Again, always make sure that students understand the text before you continue with these questions:

- Did the author remain focused on one topic? What is that topic?

Asking this question reinforces the earlier mini-lesson on focus. (I have made sure that each model from here on makes sense and is focused so students can concentrate on the craft element that is the subject of the mini-lesson.) For this piece, students should tell you that the author did stay focused on describing the different steps involved in putting new oil in a car.

Teacher: Great, the author has accomplished one of his goals. Now, let's look at vocabulary.

Continue with these questions:

Teacher: Did the author use specific vocabulary? Which words paint a specific picture that improves meaning and interest?
(Sample #2—Set A: front two tires, parking brake, flat, empty container, motor oil pan, socket wrench, drain plug, filter, filter wrench, counterclockwise, mounting base, properly dispose, hood, motor; Sample #1—Set B: rush, sketching, silhouettes, foam, inviting, sanderlings, poke and peck, shoreline smorgasbord, tambourines, percussion band.)
Let's circle these words to see how many precise vocabulary words the author used in this paragraph. (Ask students to identify precise language; circle words on the transparency.)
Are there any words that are too general and interfere with meaning or interest?
(Sample #1—Set A: front of the car, brake, empty pan, tool, area, get rid of, top of the car, hole, underneath; Sample #2—Set B: move, making pictures, birds, come and eat)
Let's underline these words to show that a better word choice would improve the quality of this piece.

Repeat the process outlined above for sample #2 of Set A (page 19). (Answers above are given for Sets A and B for space considerations, but I would suggest using only one set of samples per mini-lesson. Save the second set for another time—maybe as a refresher when you see attention dwindling on strong vocabulary.)

After discussing both samples, ask students which of the two uses more precise vocabulary. They will tell you that in Set A, sample #2 has vocabulary that is more specific and exact.

At this point in the lesson, discuss the importance of using correct terminology when writing in a specific content area. Just as the exact automotive terms added meaning to "How to Change the Oil in a Car," so, too, do accurate history, social studies, health, or math terms add meaning and interest to those kinds of pieces, as well.

Students will tell you that the first poem, sample #1 in Set B, has the most precise vocabulary because it paints stronger images in the minds of the readers. We want students to be aware that word choice is important in all forms of writing, whether we write poetry, how-to's, stories, persuasive arguments, letters, informational pieces, or personal narratives.

Discussion Points

If students cannot tell you why sample #2 in Set A or sample #1 in Set B is stronger, ask these questions:

- Which piece uses the more specific vocabulary?
- Do these words make the writing more interesting? How?
- Do these words add more meaning? How?
- Which words in sample #2, Set A are stronger than sample #1, Set A?
- Which words in sample #1, Set B are stronger than sample #2, Set B?

Clarify Vocabulary: An Overview of the Craft Element

1. Specific vocabulary helps place an exact image in the reader's mind:

   Set A: *Parking brake* is more specific than *brake*.

          Socket wrench is more specific than *tool*.

          Mounting base is more specific than *area*.

          Oil plug is more specific than *plug*.

   Set B: *Sanderlings* is more specific than *birds*.

          Tambourines is more specific than *noisemakers*.

          Sketching silhouettes is more specific than *making pictures*.

          Poke and peck is more specific than *come and eat*.

2. Specific vocabulary adds meaning by giving the reader more detail:

   Sample #2, Set A: *Remove the used oil filter by turning the filter wrench counterclockwise* tells the reader which filter, which tool is needed to remove it, and how it needs to be turned.

Sample #1, Set B: *Waves rush in/sketching silhouettes/of sky and clouds/ in foam and sand* tells the reader the movement of the waves, that they make a quick picture through sketching, that they sketch outlines of the sky and clouds, and that they do this with foam and sand.

TIPS FOR WRITERS

What Can You Do to Use More Specific Vocabulary?

1. Use a dictionary, thesaurus, or glossary to find more specific language.

2. Make a list of vague or general words that could weaken your writing. Avoid using these words as much as possible. The list may include *move, went, good, put, nice,* or *get.*

3. Make your own list of new, specific words that you would like to use in future drafts. Place this list in your writer's notebook or writing folder.

4. Set yourself a goal to include at least five specific words in each paragraph that you write.

5. Read your first draft, one sentence at a time, and circle all of the precise words that you find. Underline any vague words, and when you've finished reading, return to each and replace with a sharper, more specific word.

6. Ask a friend to read your first draft and underline in colored pencil any weak vocabulary so that you can improve it during revision.

How to Change the Oil in a Car **1**

To change the oil in a car, first drive the front of the car on ramps, pull the brake, and turn off the car. Push an empty pan under the motor oil pan. Use a tool to remove the plug. Let all of the oil drain into the pan until it stops. Take the used filter out by turning it with the tool. With a clean rag, wipe all oil and dirt from around the area. Put on the new filter. Wipe the plug clean and put it back in. Carefully pull the pan of old oil from under the car. Get rid of the used oil and filter. Raise the top of the car and twist off the oil cap. Pour new oil into the hole. Put the cap back on and shut the top of the car. Take off the brake and back off the ramps. Shut off the car and look underneath in case the oil is leaking.

Changing the Oil in a Car **2**

To change the oil in a car, first drive the front two tires up on ramps, set the parking brake, and turn off the motor. Slide a flat, empty container under the motor oil pan. Using a socket wrench, remove the drain plug. Let all of the oil in the car flow into the container until it stops dripping. Remove the used oil filter by turning the filter wrench counterclockwise. With a clean rag, wipe all oil and dirt from the mounting base. Screw on the new oil filter. Wipe the drain plug clean and screw it back in with a socket wrench. Carefully pull the container of oil out from under the car. Properly dispose of the used oil and oil filter. Raise the hood of the car and remove the oil filler cap. Pour the proper amount of new oil into the motor. Replace the cap and shut the hood of the car. Release the parking brake and slowly back off the ramps. Shut off the motor and check underneath the car for leaks around the oil plug and filter.

1

Waves Rush In and Out

waves rush
    in
     and out

waves rush in
sketching silhouettes
of sky and clouds
in foam and sand

waves rush out
inviting sanderlings
to poke and peck
the shoreline smorgasbord

waves rush in
     and out
shaking shells
like tiny tambourines
in a percussion band

waves rush
    in
     and out

2

Waves Move In and Out

waves move
    in
     and out

waves move in
making pictures
of sky and clouds
on the beach

waves move out
letting birds
come and eat
food they left in the sand

waves move in
     and out
shaking shells
like little noisemakers
in a band

waves move
    in
     and out

Developing Thorough Ideas and Information

THE QUESTION TO EXPLORE

Do the Details Thoroughly Explain the Topic?

Every reader enjoys an interesting narrative or informative essay. What elements draw a reader into the writing? Rich details, for one—fascinating facts, thoughtful quotes, or vivid descriptions that tell the reader something he or she didn't know beforehand. Students know the difference between engaging and boring writing. They want to support their ideas with specific details and information. They want their writing to pop and grab the reader's attention. You can help them recognize that the use of specific terms, dates, descriptions, or actions can develop their topic in such a way that readers will be surprised and satisfied.

Introducing the Craft Element:
Developing Thorough Ideas and Information

Begin your mini-lesson on developing thorough ideas and information like this:

Teacher: If you were given a choice between viewing a short video summary or the full-length presentation of the newest action movie in town, which would you want to watch?

Student: I'd want to see the whole movie. The short video wouldn't have all the good scenes.

Student: I'd want to see the whole thing so I could talk to my friends about all of the great parts.

Teacher: So, you don't think that summaries have a lot of great parts?

Students: No.

Teacher: Why not?

Student: Because a summary just tells you the general story. It doesn't give you any of the details. You'd miss out on all the great action scenes.

Teacher: And do you like details?

Student: Sure, that's the good stuff—that's what makes it interesting.

Teacher: I feel the same way. Details add interest to movies, books, art, and music. Details are the elaborate bits that pull us deeper into the meaning of the piece. Let's look at three written samples on the overhead and think about how each one develops ideas and information with specific details.

Discussing the Craft Element:
Developing Thorough Ideas and Information

Place sample #1 (page 25) of the *Developing Thorough Ideas and Information* transparencies on the overhead projector. Read it out loud with expression. Afterward, ask these questions:

- Do you understand what the author has written? Does it make sense?

Again, always make sure that the students understand the text before you continue with this question:

- Did the author remain focused on one topic? What is that topic?

The students will tell you that the author did stay focused on describing the importance of fossil clues in learning about the earliest life on Earth.

After you establish that the author has accomplished two of her goals, creating meaning and maintaining focus, invite students to look at vocabulary. Since we want to reinforce the idea that specific vocabulary helps build meaning and interest, I suggest a quick review of a few of the strongest words in each piece of writing. Students may point to these words and phrases: *fossils; paleontologists; stone remains; geological changes; Precambrian; stromatolites; Australia; bacteria; algae; four billion years ago; corals; trilobites; brachiopods; crinoids; oxygen-rich; jawless fish; first internal, bony skeleton; jigsaw puzzle.*

Then you can begin exploring how the writer developed the ideas and information in this paragraph. Continue the discussion with these questions:

- Are there specific details about early life in this paragraph?

- Which phrases or sentences give you thorough ideas or information— maybe even more than you knew before reading this?
  (*Sample #1: Paleontologists, scientists who study fossils; Paleontologists find, assemble, measure, date, compare, and analyze the stone remains; different plants and animals lived during the geological changes of our planet; stromatolites prove the existence of single-celled bacteria and algae almost four billion years ago; animals of the warm, ancient seas . . . corals, trilobites, brachiopods, and crinoids; lived in oxygen-rich waters from 440–570 million years ago; jawless fish developed the first internal, bony skeleton.*)

- Do these details add interest to this piece of writing? How?
  (*These details tell us the many processes that paleontologists go through to identify and date fossils. Further information names exact animals that lived on the planet. The dates help give the reader a time frame for the different kinds of life. The reader learns that this is not a complete record, but something that is pieced together through discoveries.*)

- Which words or phrases are not specific and add no thorough information?
  (*Sample #2—special scientists, long ago, near the end of this time. Sample #3—many people; many, many years ago; long, long ago.*)

Circle the words or phrases students identify as adding thorough information to show how many there are in the paragraph.

Repeat the process outlined above for the other two samples (page 26; answers for all three samples are given above for space considerations). After you've read and discussed all three, students should tell you that #1 is the most detailed and developed of the three. For that piece, they should be able to circle many details that add to the thorough development of information. They may also tell you that sample #3 lacks detail, seems vague, and offers only general information. At this point in the discussion, ask the students which way they are going to write in the future. They will no doubt reject samples #2 and #3 as models to imitate and state that they will always include specific information as in sample #1.

(These samples would provide a good review of how to thoroughly respond to essay questions on content tests. You might want to stress the point that thorough explanation gives the reader new and interesting information or ideas. Student achievement will improve when you remind them that their responses need to include specific terms, dates, descriptions, and actions.)

Discussion Points

If students cannot tell you why sample #1 is more well-developed, ask these questions:

- Which piece uses the most specific details and explanations?
- How do these details add interest to the piece? (Point to two or three different details in sample #1.)
- Which words or phrases in sample #1 offer us more information than we get in sample #3?
- How does the strong vocabulary in sample #1 add to the details in that selection?

Clarify Development of Thorough Ideas and Information: An Overview of the Craft Element

1. Specific terms, dates, descriptions, and actions help develop thorough ideas and information:
   Sample #1 uses terms such as *paleontologists* and *Precambrian*. It offers specific time frames such as *four billion years ago* and *440–570 million years ago*. This sample describes the ancient, warm ocean animals as having hard shells.

2. Develop your ideas or information in a sequential or orderly system. Sample #1 introduces the concept of the earliest recorded life on Earth and then starts recognizing fossil evidence from 4 billion years ago and proceeds forward in time.

TIPS FOR WRITERS

What Can You Do to Include More Thorough Ideas and Information?

1. Research, review, and create a rough plan before writing. Include notes for interesting details and examples in your plan.

2. Read two to three sentences silently to yourself and ask if you can add more specific terms, dates, descriptions, or actions to create a more interesting piece.

3. Read your piece to a friend and ask, "Is this writing interesting? What details or explanations helped develop what I am trying to say? Which ideas need more explanation?"

4. Have a friend read what you've written and ask, "Do you have three questions about the details or explanations?" Decide if you would like to add that information to your writing.

Early Life on Earth ⬤ 1

Clues to the earliest life on Earth are found in fossils. Paleontologists, scientists who study fossils, find, assemble, measure, date, compare, and analyze the stone remains of prehistoric life. Their findings show that different plants and animals lived during the geological changes of our planet. Precambrian life is explored in the stromatolites of Australia that prove the existence of single-celled bacteria and algae almost four billion years ago. The animals of the warm, ancient seas can be pictured in a scientist's mind after holding fossils of corals, trilobites, brachiopods, and crinoids. These hard-shelled animals lived in oxygen-rich waters from 440–570 million years ago. During this time, jawless fish developed the first internal, bony skeleton. Creating an accurate record of the earliest life is like putting a jigsaw puzzle together without all of the pieces. But as paleontologists discover new fossils and date them, more and more of the picture becomes complete.

Early Life on Earth 2

Clues to the earliest life on Earth are found in fossils. Special scientists find, date, and study fossils. Their findings show that different plants and animals lived on our planet over the years. They find fossils that prove there were bacteria and algae long, long ago.

They also find corals, trilobites, brachiopods, and crinoids. These hard-shelled animals lived in warm oceans long before dinosaurs roamed the earth. Near the end of this time, jawless fish swam the seas. Each fossil adds more information to the expanding record of early life-forms.

Early Life On Earth 3

Clues to the earliest life on Earth are found in fossils. Many people find and date fossils. That helps them learn what kinds of plants and animals lived here many, many years ago.

At first there were only single-celled animals. Later, animals, like corals, developed hard shells. These animals lived in warm oceans. Then, jawless fish swam in the oceans. They were one of the first animals to have a bony skeleton inside their bodies. It's hard to put together a record of early life on our planet. But each fossil helps people learn a little bit more about what life looked like long, long ago.

Fluency

THE QUESTION TO EXPLORE

Does One Thought or Idea Flow into Another?

As students become proficient readers, their oral language patterns become more sophisticated. They soon abandon the short, choppy sentences of their early literacy and develop the natural cadence of conversational language. Written language can duplicate the syntax and rhythm of spoken language. When this happens, thoughts and ideas flow from one to another. Writers use varied sentence structures, transitional phrases, and conjunctions to string their ideas and information together. Just as a river sometimes flows uninterrupted for a great distance, then drops over a fall, takes a sharp curve, flows over rocks, or eddies off to the side, fluent language mixes different sentence structures and lengths to create an emotional, aesthetic journey for the reader.

Introducing the Craft Element: Fluency

Begin your mini-lesson on fluency like this:

Teacher: Can anyone describe the way a river moves?

Student: It runs across the land.

Student: It gets bigger and flows faster as smaller rivers join it.

Student: Sometimes rivers are wide and move slowly; sometimes they flood and rush across the ground.

Student: Some rivers run straight, and others twist through hills and valleys.

Teacher: You've described quite a few different ways that rivers move: *fast, slow, twisty, straight, rushing, running, flowing.* That's great because no two rivers are just alike. But if you had to think of one feature that they all have in common, what would that be?

Student: They're all made of water.

Student: They all move toward lower ground; some go all the way to the ocean.

Student: The water in a river never stops; it is always moving from one place to another.

Teacher: Perfect! Just like a river is always flowing from one place to another, your writing needs to flow. Instead of being made of water, your writing is made of words. Your words, and the sentences they make, need to help your ideas and information flow from one to another. And, you mentioned that every river is different. That's true about writing. No two pieces of writing are ever the same. Each writer has a style that affects fluency. Some pieces will have a fast, almost frenetic, pace and others will meander, taking the reader through many emotional turns. Some writing will be straightforward with just the facts and others will spin off to the side in eddies of detail. But no matter what the pace or topic, our goal is to create fluency—a natural flow from idea to idea, sentence to sentence.

Teacher: Please, listen to these sentences:

Matt studied the effects of sunlight and temperature on decaying organic material. He did this for more than eighteen weeks last summer. It was his science project. He worked hard on testing his samples. He collected data. He charted his data. He looked at his results. Then he made a conclusion. It paid

off. He won first place at the regional science fair. He won a trophy. He won a cash prize of $500. His parents were proud. Matt was, too.

How did those sentences sound to you? Did one sentence flow into another? Did they sound disconnected to you? Were you able to understand what I was saying?

Students often respond that for the most part they understood what you were saying. But the sentences didn't really flow, especially in the middle where so many sentences began with the word *he*. They may tell you that those sentences sounded silly or disconnected. They may tell you that many of these sentences could be blended into longer sentences that would sound better—smoother.

Teacher: Please, listen to these sentences:

For more than eighteen weeks last summer, Matt studied the effects of sunlight and temperature on decaying organic material for his science project. He tested samples, collected and charted data, analyzed results, and wrote his conclusion. All of his long, hard work paid off at the regional science fair. Matt was awarded first prize, which consisted of a trophy and a $500 cash prize. Matt and his parents were proud.

How did these sentences sound to you? Did one sentence flow into another? Did they sound disconnected to you? Were you able to understand what I was saying?

Students usually respond that these sentences sounded better. They could hear one sentence flowing into another. There weren't as many short sentences in this example. They might tell you that this paragraph sounds more natural, like the way a person would speak. Use this opportunity to ask them how fluent they want to be in their writing. Do they want to write like the first example or the second?

Teacher: I agree with your choices. The second example is more fluent. The words carry you from idea to idea. There was nothing jarring or disconnected in the second passage. The different kinds of sentences helped me keep my mind on what was being read. One of our writing goals is to use a variety of sentence structures to create the best meaning. Part of writing fluently is hearing the words in our heads before we write them. We can listen for the rhythm that our words and sentences make. When writing flows effortlessly, we know that it is fluent.

The Reading-Writing Connection

One of the best ways to instill the natural flow of language in your students is to continue the Read Aloud through the intermediate grades. Students will hear fluid language over and over again in a meaningful context. They will notice how varied sentence structure creates a natural cadence that resembles spoken language. Reading aloud is the best investment a teacher can make to build strong foundations for student writers.

Discussing the Craft Element: Fluency

Place sample #1 (see page 34) of the *Fluency* transparencies on the overhead projector. Read it out loud to the students with expression. Before asking questions on fluency, remember to review:

- Focus
- Thorough Development of Ideas and Information
- Vocabulary

Since these pieces are designed to only show differences in fluency, the students will tell you that the author has maintained his focus. They will be able to list a few specific pieces of vocabulary such as *dull, scraping; deep in the house; rush of cool air;* and *tiptoed*. Be sure to underline or circle these words, which helps students remember some of this vocabulary when they are searching for specific words as they write.

Continue with these questions:
- Does every sentence flow easily into the next?
- Could you hear the natural flow of spoken language?
- Were there any places where the writing sounded disconnected or abrupt?

Repeat the process outlined above for the other sample (page 35). Now ask:

- Which piece is more fluent?

Most of the students will immediately tell you that sample #2 is more fluent. Here are some of the comments you are likely to hear during discussion:

- For sample #1 (see page 34), students may say that some of the sentences flow well, especially at the beginning of the piece. But the more you read, the choppier the sentences become. They will comment that too many sentences begin with the words *Jennifer* or *she*. They notice that each thought becomes its own short sentence instead of grouping two or more thoughts together.

- For sample #2 (see page 35), students will say that these sentences flow better. They like the use of the interjection *Bam!* They comment that their eyes were reading ahead to see what was going to happen next.

- Again, the students will mention that in sample #1 there is some natural flow of language, but only bits and pieces. As soon as all of the short sentences begin, the language sounds forced. Sometimes they even laugh as you read the five sentences beginning with *Jennifer tiptoed down the last few steps* and ending with

She inched toward the kitchen doorway because they know that the language sounds artificial.

- Most of the students will tell you that sample #2 has a natural flow. Many will mention that the words take the reader faster and faster until Jennifer sees her dad.

- Students can point to many places in sample #1 where the writing sounds disconnected or abrupt. (Let students come up to the overhead and mark these interruptions with colored slashes in the text.)

- The only parts that students may consider abrupt in sample #2 are immediately following the word *silence* at the beginning and again after *Bam!*

Don't be surprised when a heated discussion develops about the purpose of using these words as is. The more sophisticated readers will not think that these words interrupt the flow. Don't try to decide who is right in the discussion, but help students see that as with all reading, much of the meaning and interpretation happens in the mind of the reader.

It is important after this discussion to ask students why they think that sample #2 is more fluent. You may want to stop this mini-lesson here for one day and save for another day a discussion about the importance of varying sentence structure and the use of transitions.

Teacher: Since you identified sample #2 as more fluent, what kinds of sentences did the author blend together to create this flow?

Student: The first sentence has a compound predicate.

Teacher: How could that help develop fluency?

Student: The author was able to combine two different things that Jennifer did into one sentence. It sounds smoother than in sample #1 where the author uses two sentences to convey the same information.

Teacher: Any other sentence structures that you'd like to mention?

Student: The author uses dialogue.

Teacher: How does that help fluency?

Student: It helps the piece sound natural. It's the way all of us talk.

Teacher: Anything else that you would like to mention?

Student: I like the use of both *Silence* and *Bam!* Each one adds something different. The *Silence* adds a pause and is the beginning of our fear for Jennifer. The *Bam!* interrupts the quiet mood and adds to the fear.

Teacher: You're mentioning lots of different kinds of sentences. Are there others that you think help make this piece fluent?

Student: I like how the author begins some sentences with words like *slowly, quietly,* and *earlier.*

Teacher: Why?

Student: It gives us some information without writing a whole sentence to tell us. The word *earlier* tells us when Jennifer forgot.

Student: I like how the author combined three sentences into one when he wrote, *She grabbed his heavy flashlight, turned it on, and inched toward the kitchen.* That flows better than the three short sentences in sample #1.

Teacher: So, do you want to write with many short and simple sentences or with a blend of many different kinds of sentences?

Students: A blend of many sentences.

Teacher: Sounds like a good writing goal. This year we will use varied sentence structures to help our thoughts and ideas flow.

"Then" Alert

This is a good time to caution your students in the overuse of the word *then*. Many students think that the use of this word keeps the reader moving through the text. Actually the word *then* should never be used more than once in a short piece of writing. I also tell students that they might try to avoid its use altogether since it really doesn't add any information and quite often it creates a dead spot in the writing. If a student has overused this word in his or her piece, you may offer this strategy. Have the student delete all of the *thens* and read the composition out loud. He or she may decide that nothing is needed to replace the omitted word, or perhaps that one or two alternatives would add necessary information. One on one, or in a small group, brainstorm other time-passing transitions that the student could use. Your list might include some of these choices: *the next day, later that day, that afternoon, in the evening, later in the week, minutes later, finally,* or *afterward.*

Discussion Points

If students cannot tell you why sample #2 is more fluent, ask these questions:

- Is this piece easy to read and understand?
- Does the writer use different kinds and lengths of sentences?
- Do the ideas and sentences flow from one to another?
- Does the language sound like the way people speak?
- Can you find sentences that combine two or more ideas?

Clarify Fluency: An Overview of the Craft Element

1. Creating a plan during prewriting helps writers sequence ideas so that they flow logically from one to another in their writing.

2. A combination of different kinds of sentences—simple, compound, and complex—forms the natural cadence of spoken and written language:

   (Sample #2: "Hello," she called. "Is anybody there?" Silence. Slowly, quietly, she stood and started down the steps. Earlier Jennifer had forgotten to turn on the downstairs lights before coming up to her bedroom. Now a pool of black swirled in front of her.)

3. Transitions, both words and phrases, carry one thought into another.

   (Sample #2: And since the front of the house was dark, I thought that you weren't home.)

TIPS FOR WRITERS

What Can You Do to Make Your Writing More Fluent?

1. Read your writing out loud and see if it has the same natural rhythm as spoken language.
2. Hear what you want to write in your head before drafting. Say your intended words out loud. Listen for fluency and expression. When the sentences sound smooth and similar to the way you speak, write them.
3. Use a blend of different kinds and lengths of sentences.
4. Either read your piece out loud to a friend or have the friend read it out loud to you. Ask that friend, "Does each sentence flow into the next? Were there any places where the flow was interrupted?"
5. Read many books and pay attention to the way the writer has arranged the words so one idea flows into another.

Intruder?

Jennifer stopped writing. She listened to a dull, scraping noise. It came from somewhere deep inside the house. "Hello," she called. "Is anybody there?" No one answered her. She stood slowly and quietly. She started down the steps. Jennifer had forgotten to turn on the downstairs lights earlier. Everything was dark in front of her. The basement door slammed. A rush of cool air swept past her. Jennifer tiptoed down the last few steps. She darted into her father's bedroom. She grabbed his heavy flashlight. She turned it on. She inched toward the kitchen doorway.

"Oh! You scared me," said her dad. He jumped back. He switched on the lights.

"I scared you?!" said Jennifer. Her hands were shaking.

"Sorry, hon. My key wouldn't work tonight. The front of the house was dark. I thought that you weren't home. I forced a basement window open and crawled in."

"Next time," said Jennifer. She caught her breath. "Just ring the doorbell."

Intruder?   2

Jennifer stopped writing and listened to the dull, scraping noise that came from somewhere deep inside the house. "Hello," she called. "Is anybody there?" Silence.

Slowly, quietly, she stood and started down the steps. Earlier, Jennifer had forgotten to turn on the downstairs lights before coming up to her bedroom. Now a pool of black swirled in front of her. Bam! The basement door slammed shut and a rush of cool air swept past her. Jennifer tiptoed down the last few steps and darted into her father's bedroom. She grabbed his heavy flashlight, turned it on, and inched toward the kitchen doorway.

"Oh! You scared me," said her dad, jumping back as he turned on the lights.

"I scared you?!" said Jennifer, her hands shaking.

"Sorry, hon. My key wouldn't work tonight. And since the front of the house was dark, I thought that you weren't home. I forced a basement window open and crawled in."

"Next time," said Jennifer catching her breath, "just ring the doorbell."

Voice

THE QUESTION TO EXPLORE

Can You Hear the Author in the Writing?

Voice is that elusive element that makes a piece of writing personal and emotional. Voice is created when the natural cadence and syntax of the author's language conveys the passion at the heart of the writing. Not only is it possible to hear and recognize voice in a strong piece of writing, it is quite easy to identify writing that has no voice, leaving the reader without a personal bridge to the author.

Writing without voice is like listening to a computer giving instructions. The information and ideas are there, but the human connection is missing. In some forms of expository writing, voice is not expected or needed. Straightforward encyclopedic entries lack voice. It's just the facts and that's fine. Information is all a reader is looking for in that type of writing. Many directions for assembling or operating machinery lack voice. Again, that's acceptable, and in most cases desirable. Readers of that material require nothing more than a logical explanation of what they need to do.

But readers expect to hear voice in narrative and expository writing. Narrative writing is, after all, one way to share the stories of our lives. Through this writing we connect with one another on an emotional level. And a reader is more likely to remember information if it is presented in an engaging way. A strong, appealing voice is one means to accomplish this.

Voice is difficult to teach. It is so much easier to *show* it to your students. As you read out loud to your class, stop occasionally and discuss the voice that you hear. The greatest *ah-ha*'s for both students and teachers come when they can hear voice and identify that elusive element together in a piece that holds importance for all of them. (See page 41 for ideas for Read Alouds perfect for exploring voice.)

Introducing the Craft Element: Voice

Begin your mini-lesson on voice like this:

Teacher: Voice in writing is the personality of the author coming through the words. You learn something about the author from the language he or she uses. Voice helps us connect with the author, which piques our interest and makes us want to read on and hear more. Listen to this passage from the book *Hope Was Here* by Joan Bauer. (Teacher reads first eight paragraphs as shown on page 38.)

Teacher: Does this opening sound like a robot talking or like a human being?

Student: Like a human being.

Student: Like someone who is happy about having a job as a waitress.

Student: A human being who wants us to know just how she feels.

Teacher: What do you know about the author from listening to this passage?

Student: That the author knows something about how people act when they're stressed out.

Student: The author knows something about the restaurant business.

Student: The author knows that a waitress has to be tough, even under pressure.

Student: The author knows how to write so that kids will want to read on—I want to hear more already.

Hope Was Here

by Joan Bauer

Somehow I knew my time had come when Bambi Barnes tore her order book into little pieces, hurled it in the air like confetti, and got fired from the Rainbow Diner in Pensacola right in the middle of lunchtime rush. She'd been sobbing by the decaf urn, having accidentally spilled a bowl of navy bean soup in the lap of a man who was, as we say in the restaurant game, one taco short of a combo platter. Gib, the day manager, was screaming at her to stop crying, which made her cry all the more, which led to the firing and her stomping out the door wailing how life wasn't fair, right in front of the hungry customers. That's when Gib turned to me.

"You want her job?"

I was a bus girl at the time, which meant I cleaned off dirty tables and brought people water and silverware. I'd been salivating for years to be a waitress.

I stood up tall. "Yes, I sure do."

"You going to cry on me, fall apart if something goes wrong?"

And I saw right then if you're going to cut the mustard in food service, you'd better know how to handle turmoil. I straightened my shoulders, did my best to look like flint.

"I'm the toughest female you've ever seen," I assured him.

"You're hired then. Take the counter."

Teacher: Yes, I agree with all of your answers. We get a sense of what the author is like from her words. Do you hear emotion in this writing?

Student: Oh sure. I hear excitement.

Student: And maybe some frustration with her job in the past.

Student: There's that emotion of "I'm not going to be a wimp—I'll be strong."

Student: But there's just a little fear in there—like she's telling her boss she's tough to convince herself.

Teacher: Sharing emotion is important in writing with voice. Would you say that this writing has voice? Did the emotion in the piece help you connect with the writer?

Student: I feel like this author is showing us how some kids want things real bad. I connect with this girl wanting that job. Yes, it's got voice.

Student: It's written like how a real kid would think; yes, I think it's got voice.

Student: The author wrote this in a way that I think it could happen. I'm not sure about voice, but the scene seems real.

Teacher: I'm going to read it again to you. Listen for any words or phrases that seems to put that real kid's voice into the writing. (Teacher reads the passage again.)

Student: "Somehow I knew my time had come . . ."

Student: She'd been sobbing by the decaf urn.

Student: "And I saw right then if you're going to cut the mustard in food service, you'd better know how to handle turmoil."

Student: "I straightened my shoulders, did my best to look like flint."

Student: "I'd been salivating for years to be a waitress."

Student: I think it all sounds like the thinking and talking of a real kid. I don't think you can pull just certain words out.

Teacher: That's the sign of a strong writer. When someone can put you in a specific place with a certain person and the writing seems real, voice is everywhere. Let's do another short example. Listen to this passage:

I gently pulled the tiny violet between my fingers. How did this flower know to grow this size, with this color and shape? How can every rose have similar petals? How is it that most lilies are the same size? How can snapdragons be identical in shape? How can that be, when here I am, a human being so

completely different from everyone around me, and I still don't know what I'm going to be?

Do you hear voice?

Student: It sounds like the way people wonder about things. It makes me feel bad for the person because you can tell this is bugging them right now.

Student: I think it has voice because it sounds real. Sometimes the smallest thing can make you think, "Hey, what about me!"

Student: It gets me thinking about that, too.

Teacher: So, there is a connection? You do feel some emotion and a tie with the author. Any time that the author, reader, and writing are pulled together with authentic language and emotion, you have voice.

Beware of Prompts

❋

Since standardized tests use prompts to engage students in the applied writing sample, teachers consider it good practice to increase the number of prompts given in the classroom. They feel they are "preparing" students for the test. Please, remember that our purpose in having students write is to learn how to communicate effectively with an audience. To do that, students need opportunities to write about what they know, feel, and think. Out of this type of personal commitment comes voice. The best preparation for any writing assessment is total engagement in meaningful writing. Give your students as much practice in writing with self-selected topics as possible. Their gained confidence and skills will help them succeed with the test.

Discussing the Craft Element: Voice

Explain to students that they will be reading letters that could run in a middle-school newspaper. Place sample #1 (page 43) of the *Voice* transparencies on the overhead projector. Read it out loud to students with expression. Before asking questions on voice, quickly review:

- Focus

- Development of Thorough Ideas and Information
- Vocabulary

Since these pieces are designed to show only differences in voice, students will tell you that the piece has focus. The development of ideas and information will vary between pieces, as will vocabulary since voice is dependent on authentic vocabulary. I encourage you to continue circling specific vocabulary to reinforce the power of thoughtful word choice.

When you're ready to begin the discussion on voice, ask these questions:

- Does this piece sound authentic? Does the language seem natural for a middle-school student?

- Do you think this piece has voice?

- Do you connect to an emotion in this piece?

- Which phrases or sentences help you connect to the author?

    (Sample #1: I believe; then we could negotiate; It's not their fault; that could be used as sealer on the space shuttle; floats in a puddle of seasoned grease on taco chips; And haven't you always wondered; So, buckle up; it's time we did our share; Notice that I didn't say eat the lunch; yeah, right; ours, not theirs; the lemonade's on me. Sample #2: Be a doer, not a whiner. Sample #3: We've got a problem here; but they don't have much to start with; So, let's help them; One thing we can do; I think that would be an eye-opening experience; to show our dissatisfaction; forced us to take severe measures; Come to our; Do it for your stomach.)

Repeat the process for the other two samples in this set (page 44). Afterward, ask the students which piece has the most voice.

Sometimes a piece of writing has some voice, as do samples #2 and #3 of this set. A reader can sense that the author is experimenting, trying to relate to the audience in a sincere way. You will notice these kinds of attempts in your students' writing. Celebrate these initial efforts; more will follow.

Discussion Points

If students cannot tell you why sample #1 has the strongest voice, then ask these questions:

- Which piece sounds most like a person speaking?

- Which piece has the most emotion? Can you identify that emotion?

- Which piece has the most phrases or indicators of authentic voice?

Don't be surprised when students tell you that sample #2 is boring and has no voice. They might say that the author attempted voice in her last line,

Literature Links

Here are some great passages in books that help support you and your students in your understanding and use of voice. Read these passages out loud together and discuss the connection you feel with the author and the writing because of the voice.

Because of Winn-Dixie by Kate DiCamillo (first two pages)

The Rifle by Gary Paulsen (the first two pages of the third section, "The Joining")

Baby by Patricia MacLachlan (the first two pages of chapter 15)

The Van Gogh Cafe by Cynthia Rylant (first two pages of "Lightning Strikes")

Out of the Dust by Karen Hesse ("The Accident")

Among the Hidden by Margaret Peterson Haddix

but it was too late. There was no other emotion or personal connection throughout her piece. They will recognize that sample #3 has voice, but it is not as easily identifiable as the voice in sample #1.

Clarify Voice: An Overview of the Craft Element

1. Natural language patterns help create voice:
   Sample #1: And haven't you always wondered what exactly is in that grainy, firm patty on surprise burger day?!

2. Personal topics lend themselves to writing with a strong voice. For example, organizing students to do something about poor cafeteria food is a topic writers may feel strongly about.

3. Sharing an emotion with the audience is part of voice. In sample #1, Patrick uses humor to make his point with his audience.

4. Writing with a sense of audience improves voice:
   Sample #1: Buy the lunch. (Notice that I didn't say eat the lunch.)

5. Sometimes a title can give a hint of the voice to come:
   Sample #1: Grease Today, Tuna Steak Tomorrow

TIPS FOR WRITERS

What Can You Do to Include Voice?

1. Write about topics that are important to you—ones that inspire you to be passionate.

2. Use words and phrases from your natural speaking vocabulary in your writing. Rely on specific vocabulary to help you show how people talk, feel, think, or act.

3. Have a friend read your writing and ask, "Can you hear me in this piece of writing? Is there emotion in what I'm writing?" (Possible emotions include wonder, humor, fear, anger, frustration, regret, joy, hesitancy, sadness, or excitement.)

4. Read your own writing out loud. Does it sound like a robot wrote some facts and ideas, or does it sound human and personal?

Celebrate Voice

The use of voice can be contagious. I look for examples of voice in student work as I tour the room for 6–8 minutes during writing time. If I notice a passage that has strong voice, I might ask the student if I may make a copy and use it as a beginning for a mini-lesson the following day. Or sometimes I politely interrupt the class and give the author a moment to read the passage out loud and we all celebrate the voice we hear.

Other times, when students are reading their pieces to peers, one or more will ask if their partner can share a portion of their writing that has strong voice. All of these mini-celebrations help create an understanding and eagerness about voice. The more students hear voice, the easier they recognize it and include it in their own writing. It's contagious.

Grease Today, Tuna Steak Tomorrow

I believe that more students should buy the school lunch. If at least 85% of the middle school population would pay for the hot lunch every day, then we could negotiate for better meals. It's difficult for the cafeteria ladies to assemble nutritional, tasty lunches on a limited budget. It's not their fault that the quality of pasta and faux dairy products they are given creates macaroni and cheese that could be used as sealer on the space shuttle. They're not pleased when the inexpensive ground beef that they're forced to serve floats in a puddle of seasoned grease on taco chips. And haven't you always wondered what exactly is in that grainy, firm patty on surprise burger day?! (I even saw one of the cafeteria ladies examining it for herself under a microscope in the science lab.) So, buckle up. If our good friends, Mrs. Hazelton and Mrs. Goodlaw, have to persevere with their inferior ingredients day in and day out, it's time we did our share. Buy the lunch. (Notice that I didn't say eat the lunch.) Boost cafeteria revenue so that next month we can persuade administration to hear our demands for double cheeseburgers and grilled tuna steak. Yeah, right!

If you want to chew the fat (ours, not theirs) about this issue some more, come to Perkins Park Saturday morning. And if you bring a better remedy than mine, the lemonade's on me.

—Patrick Holling, 7th grade

Make It Better   2

I think that more students should pay attention to the quality of our cafeteria food. It isn't very good. We need to do something to get better food. We need to get people to listen to us. It's time that students assemble and discuss our options. I would like to invite any interested people to my house on Wednesday night to talk about what we can do. Be a doer, not a whiner.

—Laura White, 7th grade

Our Cafeteria Food Needs Your Help!   3

We've got a problem here at Cumberland Middle School—the cafeteria food. It's dry, tough, and tasteless. We need to draw attention to this problem. Our cafeteria ladies try to make healthy, good lunches, but they don't have much to start with. So, let's help them. One thing we can do is write letters to the superintendent and school board members. Invite them to have lunch with us every day for a week. I think that would be an eye-opening experience. Another idea is to stage a boycott. Every student in the middle school would refuse to buy anything in the cafeteria for one month to show our dissatisfaction with the food. Somebody could call the newspaper. We could give interviews about our concerns and how the menus and quality of food have forced us to take severe measures. Come to our organizational meeting this Tuesday night at Bill's Bowling Alley at 7 o'clock. Bring your best ideas on how we can bring better food into our school. Do it for your stomach. Do it for your school!

—Amanda Waller, 7th grade

Describing Voice

What Kind of Voice Do You Hear?

Describing voice means giving a name to the tone that you hear in a piece of writing. For shorter pieces, the tone usually remains the same. For instance, if a child is writing a thank-you note to her grandmother for a family heirloom that she received for her birthday, the entire letter will probably have an appreciative and respectful tone. But in longer pieces, the voice can change depending on what is happening or the point of view. During the course of a short story, the voice can change from expectant to disappointed to determined. Again, remind students to be observant of the emotional connection they make to different pieces of writing. Read a variety of short stories or picture books aloud to your students and encourage them to describe in their own words the voice they hear. I'm always amazed how accurately they pinpoint the voice(s) that they hear. Possible descriptors of voice could be: *authoritative, pensive, whimsical, reminiscent, playful, cautionary, enthusiastic, eerie, joyful, angry, apologetic, silly, menacing,* or *loving.* The more practice you provide in listening for voice and describing it, the more you will see this element appear in your students' writing.

Introducing the Craft Element: Describing Voice

Begin your mini-lesson on describing writer's voice like this:

Teacher: Would all of us have the same feelings and reactions if we sat down right now and took an hour test on the events leading up to the Revolutionary War?

Student: I'd be panicked. I can't remember too much about what happened before the Revolutionary War.

Student: I think I'd feel good about it. I just read a novel set during that time and I remember a lot of details.

Student: I think that our feelings would be different depending on how well we did on the test.

Teacher: I think that you are probably correct. What if we sat down after the test and wrote about our feelings and how well we thought we did? Would the emotion and voice be about the same for each of us since we're all writing about the same thing?

Your students will no doubt acknowledge that a range of emotion and voice would be likely. Some in the class might consider the test fun, and their writing would be confident and full of enthusiasm. Others might be mad they'd been given a surprise test. And still others might write with an "I don't care" voice since the test was only an experiment and not a real evaluation.

Teacher: So, even though we would all be writing about the same experience, our words would be filtered through our knowledge and emotions. And, you're telling me that all of our voices could be quite different.

Students: Yes.

Teacher: When we describe voice, we put a name on that tone or sound we hear in the writing. Let me give you a quick example. Tell me how you would describe the voice in this short passage.

Every night for four months I glued toothpick to toothpick. And as of last night, my replica of a suspension bridge was almost

complete. Then, without any regard for my time or effort, my cousin pushed his hand on the top. "Let's see how strong this bridge really is," he said.

"Stop!" I ordered. But before I could cross the room to pull him away, the sound of snap, snap, snap told me much of my work had been destroyed.

How would you describe the voice that you hear in this short piece?

One student may say that the voice seems controlled, considering the anger this person must feel. Another might respond that he would describe the voice as disappointed. Still another student might say that it is a frustrated voice.

Remind students that there is not one correct answer. A reader and writer make a connection through a piece of writing. The reader brings past experiences and understandings to that reading. It is possible for many readers to describe the voice with different terms. They will all be similar, but hardly ever identical.

Discussing the Craft Element: Describing Voice

Place sample #1 (page 50) of the *Describing Voice* transparencies on the overhead projector. Read it out loud to the students with expression. Before asking students to describe the voice they hear, remember to review:

- Focus
- Development of Thorough Ideas and Information
- Vocabulary

Since these pieces are designed to only show different kinds of voices, the students will tell you that the different pieces have focus. The development of ideas and information will vary from piece to piece, as will the use of specific vocabulary. Again, encourage the students to circle strong vocabulary so that they are reminded to include precise language in all of their writing.

Continue the discussion with these questions:

- Do you hear a writer's voice in this piece?
- Does this piece engage you on some emotional level?
- What kind of voice do you hear? What words describe it?

Repeat the process outlined above with the other three samples in this set (pages 50–51). Students should tell you that they hear voice in #1, #2, and #4. They will tell you that #3 has no voice, that it is blah and sounds like "just the facts." Students will use different words to describe the voices in each piece, but they will tend to be similar. For instance, students often describe the voice in #1 as *playful*, *relaxed*, *friendly*, or *silly*. For #2, they often identify an *easy*, *calm*, *restful*, or *content* voice. Sample #4 usually receives varied responses. Some descriptions were: *annoyed*, *playful*, *loving*, *nostalgic*, or *story-like*.

Discussion Points

If students cannot describe the voice they hear in samples #1, #2, and #4, ask these questions while looking at the samples on the overhead projector.

- For Sample #1: How does the author feel about time at Rosa's pool? What words describe this feeling? How does the writing make you feel? Sad? Angry? Playful? Anxious?

- For Sample #2: How does the author feel about having these lazy days at the water? What words describe this feeling? How does this writing make you feel? Happy? Excited? Calm? Quiet?

- For Sample #4: How does the author feel about her sister Erin tagging along? Can the author still enjoy herself with Erin? What words describe the mixed feelings that she has? How does this writing make you feel? Excited? Restful? Frustrated?

Clarify Describing Voice: An Overview of the Craft Element

1. Planning during prewriting can help a writer get a sense of the voice before he or she begins the piece.

2. When a writer writes about something he or she knows or cares about, feelings come through as sincere emotion in the voice:

   Sample #1: We call it that because when you get eight or more lively kids into a pool, the water shakes, pops, squirts, and rolls and we have to snort pool water just to breathe.

   Sample #2: I'm content letting the water rock me like a baby while the sun warms my back.

   Sample #4: That's Erin—shocking. But I have to admit that summer would be a bit boring without her.

3. Specific details help create a distinct voice:

   Sample #1: Danny cannonballs, Myra and Joey play Marco Polo, and Josh is a torpedo launched from Big Max's shoulders.

   Sample #2: My body slides through the cool water with only the sound of my kicking and breathing to keep me company.

Sample #4: "Pleeeeeez, oh please, take me," she begs until I feel obliged as the compassionate older sister to invite her along.

4. Titles can help a writer introduce the voice for a piece.

   Sample #1: Water Up Your Nose

   Sample #2: Lazy Days of Summer

   Sample #4: Summer Fun Despite Erin

TIPS FOR WRITERS

What Can You Do to Include a Describable Voice?

---

1. Decide on a tone before writing. Post it on your plan and maintain that tone unless something happens in your piece to change it.

2. Let your writing reflect your true emotions about your topic. Your voice may change as your language reflects your feelings at different places in your writing.

3. Read your first draft to a friend and ask, "What kind of voice do you hear? Can you describe it?"

4. Put your writing away for a day or two. Then, reread it out loud three different times to see if you can hear and identify your own voice in your writing.

Water Up Your Nose   1

Summer is filled with do-your-chores-first-and-play-at-the-pool-later days.
Every sunny afternoon, my friend Rosa and I meet at precisely 1:30 at her
backyard gate. Pooltime! Some days it's just the two of us. We practice our
own Olympic-style dives and see how many laps we can swim before one of us
begs for mercy. But most days Rosa calls a bunch of neighborhood kids for
water-up-your-nose fun. We call it that because when you get eight or more
lively kids into a pool, the water shakes, pops, squirts, and rolls and we have to
snort pool water just to breathe. Danny cannonballs, Myra and Joey play
Marco Polo, and Josh is a torpedo launched from Big Max's shoulders. Rosa
and I deep-sea dive and surprise Amanda hanging on the rope. Splash!
Wham! Kick! Slam! Splash! Rosa's pool is waves of fun!

Lazy Days of Summer   2

When summer begins, it's lazy days at the water for me. I like to start the
day by rowing out to a calm spot in Lake Blossom and dropping my line. I
listen to the caw of the birds in distant trees and the lapping of the water
against the side of the boat. If I happen to catch a pike or two, it's a lovely
reward. If not, I'm content letting the water rock me like a baby while the sun
warms my back. Later in the day I slip into the lake to swim laps in front of
the beach. My body slides through the cool water with only the sound of my
kicking and breathing to keep me company. In the evenings, I float on an air
mattress and watch the sun splash the sky with pastel watercolors. Summer
and water—it's the best therapy for me.

Summer and Water 3

I look forward to summer so that I can spend lots of time in the water. I like to canoe and fish. These are quiet times when I can think and listen to the sounds around me. When it gets really hot outside I ride my bike to the pool near our house. The water is always cool so I stay in and swim laps or float on my back. Eventually my body feels cold all the way through. Some days I set up the sprinkler for the little kids in the neighborhood. They enjoy it and it does take the edge off the heat for an afternoon. But probably the best summer water is an August rain. It rinses all of the dust and heat off the grass, buildings, streets, and me. Like I said, I look forward to summer and the time I can spend in water.

Summer Fun Despite Erin 4

Summer means lake cottage and lake cottage means water fun, unless my sister Erin is nearby. If I load up the rowboat for a morning fishing trip, there she is. "Pleeeeeez, oh please, take me," she begs until I feel obliged as the compassionate older sister to invite her along. Big mistake. She never sits still, always talks too loudly, and refuses to bait her own hook. As soon as her tummy growls, I hear "Pleeeeeez, oh please, row me back now." Later in the day, I might swim laps back and forth in front of our beach, building endurance for the swim team. Splash! A pile of gooey seaweed lands right on my head. Giggles turn into glubs as Erin dunks out of sight. By far, her worst prank involves me on the air mattress. I'm covered in sunscreen, floating, almost asleep, with my hands dangling in the water, when she sneaks up under me and pinches my fingertips. YEOW! My arms jerk up and I slide into the lake, flailing upside down. Erin grabs the air mattress and paddles away. Eventually, I swim back to shore in a state of shock! That's Erin—shocking. But I have to admit that summer would be a bit boring without her.

Show, Don't Tell

Does the Writing Show What's Happening?

Show, don't tell. We hear that advice often enough, but what does it really mean? It means that a writer's words need to paint a picture or create a movie in the mind of the reader. He or she will see what's happening, hear the words, and feel the sensations described by the writer. It's easy to *tell* an audience what happened. But it takes more thoughtful reflection to carefully select verbs, metaphors, similes, sensory details, descriptions, or feelings to *show* a firsthand account of an event. When an author *shows*, the writing provides the reader with an intimate view. Telling keeps the reader at a distance. We want to help our students know the difference between the two and make a conscious effort to show as much as they can in their writing.

Introducing the Craft Element: Show, Don't Tell

Begin your mini-lesson on *show, don't tell* like this:

Teacher: Please shut your eyes and listen to this sentence:

> **Mavis was angry when she heard what the umpire said.**

Now, show me through a series of actions what you saw in your mind.

This beginning to the lesson provides an opportunity for students to role play what they understand from the sentence. Their actions will vary. Some will shake their fist. Others might kick their leg or throw their arms up. Some might scowl or show other facial clues for the anger. But, of course, there won't be much action because the sentence is distant and telling.

Teacher: Please shut your eyes again and listen to this sentence:

> **Shaking her head back and forth, Mavis pounded home plate with her fist after the umpire shouted, "You're out!"**

Again, show me what you saw in your mind.

If the students were listening attentively, their first question might be whether or not two of them could act this out. One would assume the role of the umpire; the other would become Mavis.

You'll notice that if several students act this out, their movements will be quite similar because the sentence shows us specifically what happened.

Teacher: Which sentence *showed* you Mavis's anger? Which sentence offered you the most details? Which sentence painted the most specific picture in your mind?

Students will agree that the second sentence painted a clearer picture. Point out that showing what happened, rather than simply telling the information, is what makes all the difference. Strategies writers use to show what is happening include:

- Describing the character's actions rather than just saying how he or she feels.
- Using active verbs.
- Describing a specific setting.
- Using similes and metaphors to create images.
- Using dialogue.
- Showing what the character is thinking.
- Appealing to some of the five senses to paint a picture of what is happening.

Class Demonstration:

❊

Revising Tell to Show

Students need to see how to revise a telling sentence into a showing sentence. I like to model this activity in front of the students on the overhead projector. For instance, I write a telling sentence like this one: **The girl cried a lot.** Next, I ask the students, "Describe the picture that this sentence paints in your mind." Responses will vary because the sentence uses vague language. The students quickly determine that it doesn't show us much, it only offers a general view of what happened through a telling.

Continue with the demonstration with the words: Before I begin to brainstorm other ways to write this with more show, I ask them:

What are more specific words I could use for girl?

They might respond with *teenager, princess, toddler, salesgirl, daughter,* or a specific girl's name. I put these in a list.

I would then ask, *What are some other more specific words that mean* cry?

They might say, *whimpered, sobbed, bawled, wailed, wept,* or *blubbered.* I put these on a separate list.

Finally, I would ask for other ways to say *a lot.* Their answers would vary considerably on this, but I jot some of these down as well. Then, incorporating their suggestions, I write three to four sentences that show this action:

The teenager threw herself on her bed and sobbed into her pillow until she fell asleep.

The toddler bawled uncontrollably when the storekeeper took the display doll out of her hands.

The princess whimpered into her handkerchief when she realized that she had dropped her ring into the raging river.

I like to demonstrate how we can derive many meanings from the first sentence, but that each of my showing sentences paints a specific picture. When we model for the students—both thinking out loud and writing—it gives them a template for how they need to think and revise telling sentences into showing sentences in their own writing.

For further practice at another time you might give your students one of these telling sentences and have them rewrite it as a sentence that shows instead. I've done this with quite a few classes and the students enjoy sharing their different revisions out loud with one another. It truly amazes them how many meaningful variations can be created from one boring sentence.

The boy nervously waited for the bus. (What did his body do?)

The cat did the trick correctly. (Describe the cat's actions.)

The river went over its banks. (Use a more specific verb.)

The deliveryman ran from the dog. (Describe what he did and identify the dog.)

The man chewed the meat. (What did the man's mouth and teeth do?)

The tired lady walked toward her home. (What did her body do?)

The teacher was frustrated. (How did she display her frustration?)

The flower blew in the wind. (Use specific vocabulary and describe how it blew.)

After just a little practice, students will surprise you by paying much more attention to this kind of detail in their own writing. They will help one another identify telling sentences during peer critique sessions. *Show, don't tell* will become part of their everyday author talk.

Let the Emotions Show

❋

Quite often student authors will write these kinds of sentences: *She was afraid. He was very angry. They were disappointed. My sister was sad.* Address these kinds of sentences straight on. Let the students know that authors try to **show** emotion, rather than **tell** emotion. I always ask the students to describe for me what their bodies do when they are afraid. The variety of responses includes: *my heart beats fast, my legs wobble, my hands get sweaty, I scream and run, I bite my lips, my whole body trembles,* and *my stomach hurts.* I then explain that this is the type of detail that *shows* fear. These details place a reader at the scene and paint a picture in his or her mind. Readers want to know what the person did when she was afraid, lonely, disappointed, sad, or angry. Our standard questions are: **What did his body do? What did her body do? What did their bodies do?** Asking these simple questions is a great tool to help students *show* emotion, not *tell*.

Discussing the Craft Element: Show, Don't Tell

Place sample #1 (page 58) of the *Show, Don't Tell* transparencies on the overhead projector. Read it out loud to the students with expression. Before asking students to discuss *show, don't tell* please remember to review:

- Focus
- Development of Thorough Ideas and Information
- Vocabulary

Since these pieces are designed to only show the difference between *show* and *tell*, the students should tell you that the different pieces have focus. The development of ideas and information will vary from piece to piece, as well as the amount of specific vocabulary. Again, encourage the students to circle specific words so that they may add them to their working vocabularies.

Now, ask these questions to help students identify phrases that are examples of showing rather than telling:

- Active verbs help to show, rather than tell. Which verbs grab your attention and take you into this scene? (*Sample #3: pump, press, brushes, loops, carrying, flash, races, veers, jumping, beats.*)

- Which verbs seem blah and don't help you paint a picture in your mind? (*Sample #1: touches, goes, ride, flies, pulls. Sample #2: move, hits, goes, are, is, goes, moves.*)

- Do you see or feel any of the author's experiences from this writing? Which images pull you into this bike ride? (*Sample #3: my head pushed forward like the bow of a boat; I pump my bike fast and hard; Whoosh! My tires press against the hot blacktop; cool air brushes my face; Like a ribbon, the bike path loops; carrying me effortlessly over hills and around curves; autumn trees flash a colorful border; songbird races alongside me; The sun plays peek-a-boo; jumping out from shadows; My heart beats in rhythm with my pedals.*)

- Which images are uninteresting and keep you from entering the scene? (*Sample #1: pedal my bike real hard, cool wind touches my face, bike path goes around, I ride over hills and around curves, Lots of fall trees, past my eyes, until he gets tired and pulls away, as fast as my feet pedal. Sample #2: pedal fast, My tires move over the pavement, the wind hits my face, path goes around, Many colorful trees are on my sides, A bird is next to me, it goes away, The sun moves, It's fun, My heart goes fast, so do my feet.*)

Repeat the process with the other two samples in this set (pages 58–59). Afterward, ask students which piece does the most showing. It can be helpful to place each transparency on the overhead one more time for a quick review.

Discussion Points

If students cannot tell you why sample #3 is the strongest example of *show, don't tell*, ask these questions while showing that sample on the overhead projector:

- Find a phrase that makes you feel as if you can see or feel what the bike rider is experiencing.
- How does the author describe the surroundings?
- What are three specific verbs the author uses to pull you into the piece?
- Are there any phrases or sentences that seem dull or distant?

Clarify Show, Don't Tell: An Overview of the Craft Element

1. Show the reader what is happening with specific, active verbs: *pump, press, brushes, loops, flash,* and *races.*

2. Paint pictures in the mind of the reader with precise language: *like the bow of a boat; like a ribbon, the bike path loops; autumn trees flash a colorful border just outside my focus.*

3. Include indicators of emotion: *Push. Speed. Exhilaration; this is what freedom feels like today.*

4. Include the thoughts or feelings of a character, if possible: *this is what freedom feels like today.*

5. Add dialogue to take the reader to the scene when there is more than one character.

6. Eliminate any uninteresting words or phrases; make every word count.

TIPS FOR WRITERS

What Can You Do to Include More Show, Not Tell?

1. Use images that appeal to the five senses.
2. Describe what a person does, instead of saying what feeling he or she has.
3. Select strong, active verbs that help paint a picture in the reader's mind.
4. Include the actual thoughts or words spoken when you can.
5. Read your writing to a friend and ask, "Can you find at least four places where my writing is showing this scene to the reader?"
6. Use similes or metaphors wherever possible to enhance the imagery.

Freedom   1

I lean forward and pedal my bike real hard into the park. My tires zoom over the hot blacktop and the cool wind touches my face. The bike path goes around the picnic area, the golf course, and along the river. I ride over hills and around curves. Lots of fall trees flash past my eyes. A bird flies alongside me, until he gets tired and pulls away. The sun peeks in and out of shadows. My heart beats as fast as my feet pedal. This is freedom.

Freedom   2

I lean forward on my bike and pedal fast. My tires move over the pavement and the wind hits my face. The path goes around the picnic area, golf course, and river. Many colorful trees are on my sides. A bird is next to me, but then it goes away. The sun moves in and out of shadows. It's fun. My heart goes fast and so do my feet. Freedom.

Freedom Ride   3

   With my head pushed forward like the bow of a boat, I pump my bike fast and hard into the park. Whoosh! My tires press against the hot blacktop, while cool air brushes my face. Like a ribbon, the bike path loops around the picnic area, through the golf course, and along the river, carrying me effortlessly over hills and around curves. Acres of autumn trees flash a colorful border just outside my focus. A songbird races alongside me, but soon falls behind and veers into the woods. The sun plays peek-a-boo jumping out from shadows right in front of me. Push. Speed. Exhilaration. My heart beats in rhythm with my pedals and I realize that this is what freedom feels like today.

Organization

Does the Writing Have a Beginning, Middle, and End?

Whether it's a poem, personal narrative, persuasive argument, letter, fictional story, or informational piece, all writing needs a beginning, middle, and end. Each of these organizational parts serves a purpose. The beginning introduces the subject, entices the reader to continue, and sets the tone. The middle supplies the reader with all of the interesting details, the imagery, or facts that develop the ideas introduced in the beginning. The ending pulls everything together in a satisfying conclusion for the reader. The organization helps the reader know what to expect, and it also helps the author remain focused and construct a meaningful piece of writing. But organization doesn't just happen. We need to present student writers with different strategies so they can learn to organize their thoughts on paper or in their heads before they write.

Introducing the Craft Element: Organization

Begin your mini-lesson on organization like this:

Teacher: Can anyone explain what happens when you order a large meal including appetizer, salad, main dish, side dish, drink, and dessert? How is that food presented to you after it is prepared?

Students will offer varying opinions, but eventually they will establish that first the appetizer is served. Then, in many restaurants the salad is the next course brought to the table. The main dish and side dish are served at the same time with the drink. After the meal, the dessert is brought to the diner. Students will generally agree on this order.

Teacher: Why is it served in that order? Is there a reason it's done that way?

Again, there will be many comments from the students. But through their discussion they will likely surmise that the appetizer is brought out to curb the hunger while the diner waits for the rest of the meal.

Teacher: So, the only purpose of the appetizer is to keep the diner from getting too hungry while the chef prepares the meal?

Students will then tell you that it also prepares the diner for the meal. It's just a little something to nibble on. And, someone will mention how the appetizers are always really tasty—a special treat. Someone might even say that it gets the diner ready or excited to taste the rest of the meal.

Teacher: So, let me review all of this. You say that the appetizer is a small portion of something really good that is served while the rest of the meal is being prepared. And it also helps get you excited about the rest of the meal. Is that correct? Now, what is the purpose of the salad, main dish, side dish and drink?

There will be many comments again. But it will distill down to this: the salad, main dish, side dish, and drink are many separate flavors and foods that fill you up.

Teacher: You're saying that these different parts of the meal satisfy the hunger of the diner. They give the diner what he or she needs to feel better. Is that correct? What, then, is the purpose of the dessert?

There will be animated discussion that boils down to this: dessert is the best part of the meal.

Teacher: Why is dessert the best part?

They will mention how it is usually a rather small piece of something sweet. It makes the meal complete.

Teacher: You feel that the dessert completes the meal, but it is quite different from the main dish. Is that correct?

I agree with everything you have said. And, I think we can use that same model when we think about the beginning, middle, and end of a piece of writing. The beginning is the appetizer. It's something small, but appealing, that entices the reader into the main, or middle, part of the writing. The beginning, like the appetizer, gets you ready for the main part, the middle.

The middle of a piece of writing resembles the salad, main dish, side dish, and drink. It's the real substance of the writing. It's the part that fills us up with specific ideas and information. It's the part that takes away our hunger for ideas and information.

The ending of a piece of writing plays the same role as dessert. It rounds out the piece, adds to it, and pulls it together. After a good ending, a reader is satisfied and feels like the writing is complete.

Classroom Support

❋

If you introduce beginning, middle, and end to your students as I have described above, you might want to have students help you design a large poster or bulletin board that will remind them of the purposes of each organizational part. For the display, you could choose to represent anything with three parts, preferably something in which parts one and three would be smaller than part two. For instance, one model often used is that of a sandwich: two slices of bread and several items in between. So, if you had a student draw one slice of bread on top, you could label that the beginning. If you were writing informational pieces at the time, you could label it topic sentence(s). Next to or under the word *beginning* you could list these:

- opening sentence(s)
- provides a preview of the content and tone of the writing
- makes the reader want to continue on

Each of the sandwich makings is another idea or piece of information, hopefully detailed. In the diagram you could have leafy lettuce, sliced tomato, a layer of pickles, ham, cheese, and a condiment. Next to or under the word *middle* you could put:

- several ideas or pieces of information with details
- explains or develops the topic introduced in the beginning

The bottom slice of bread would be labeled as the ending, or for informational writing, the conclusion. Next to or under the word *ending* you could post:

- pulls the piece of writing together
- satisfies the reader

This type of visual reminder can be supportive as the student constructs a plan or the actual first draft of a piece of writing.

As an extension, either now or in a later mini-lesson, I like to put one transparency of either a short newspaper article, an informational piece, a poem, or a picture book story on the overhead projector. Together, the class decides exactly what sentence(s) make the beginning of the piece. Then we move to the end of the piece and they decide what sentence(s) make the ending. We mark the beginning with a large "B" and show where it starts and ends with slash marks. We mark the ending with a large "E" and show where it starts and ends with slash marks. Everything else is the middle. This is a great visual support for those students who have difficulty understanding the construction of beginning, middle, and end.

B /Millions of seahorses are plucked from the oceans each year./

M Some are sold as tropical fish for aquariums. Most are dried and used as

M medicines or as souvenirs. However, some trade management programs have

M been successful. A few countries have placed seahorses under their wildlife

M protection plans. Other countries are beginning to monitor the numbers traded

M each year. Some countries are establishing sanctuaries where seahorses are

M protected under no-fishing laws.

E /As with all preservation efforts, change is slow. But with education and new legislation, seahorses will remain in our oceans into the future./

Discussing the Craft Element: Organization

Place sample #1 (page 67) of the *Organization* transparencies on the overhead projector. Read it out loud to the class with expression. Before asking students to discuss organization, please remember to review:

- Focus
- Development of Thorough Ideas and Information
- Vocabulary

Since these pieces are designed to only show the different levels of organization, the students should tell you that all of the pieces have focus. The development of ideas and information will vary from piece to piece, as well as the amount of specific vocabulary. Continue to encourage your students to underline the vocabulary that they think adds interest to the writing. Now ask these questions:

- Does this piece have a beginning? What sentence(s) give us a taste of what the rest of the writing will offer?
  (Sample #1 and #2: The famous duel between Alexander Hamilton and Aaron Burr is a part of American history.)
- Does this piece have a middle? How many different pieces of information explain, or support, the topic in the beginning?
  (Sample #1: five pieces of information and explanation. Sample #2: fourteen pieces of information and explanation. Sample #3 has no real beginning, but there are ten pieces of information.)
- Does this piece have a conclusion? Which sentence(s) pull the piece together and satisfy you as a reader?
  (Sample #1: There is a poor conclusion, which is tacked on—it does not flow as a natural ending from the rest of the piece: Dueling is illegal in the United States today. Sample #2: This was America's most famous duel, but by no means its last. Slowly, individual states outlawed the practice and today dueling with deadly weapons is illegal everywhere in the United States. Sample #3: this piece has no ending.)

Repeat the process outlined above with the other two samples in this set (pages 67–68). After examining all three pieces, ask the students which piece has the most developed beginning, middle, and end. To help the students recognize the strongest piece, you can label the beginnings, middles, and ends as you read each one independently. Then students will need to see each piece again briefly on the overhead projector to identify #2 as the most organized.

Discussion Points

If students cannot tell you that sample #2 is the strongest in organization, ask these questions while showing that piece on the overhead projector:

- Which sentence(s) tell you what this piece is going to be about?
- Do you want to continue after reading this beginning? Do you want to hear more information and explanation?
- Which sentence(s) end this piece?
- Does this ending pull this piece of writing to a conclusion?
- Does this ending satisfy you?
- How many different pieces of information or explanation can you find in the middle of this piece?
- Do these three parts make sense to you? Did you read information in an understandable way?

Clarify Organization: An Overview of the Craft Element

1. Make a simple plan on paper before writing your first draft. In just a few words, organize what ideas or information you want to place in the beginning, middle, and end. The author of sample #2, for example, might have sketched a few notes like these:

   B: Ham. & Burr—duel—Amer. history

   M: info on two men; political enemies; purpose of duel back then; Burr challenged Ham.; NJ allowed dueling; Ham. did not want to kill; Burr fired; not prosecuted

   E: dueling in America, then and now

2. Strong beginnings have three different purposes. First, they let the reader know what the piece is about. **The famous duel between Alexander Hamilton and Aaron Burr . . .** Second, a beginning sets the tone for the piece. **The famous duel between Alexander Hamilton and Aaron Burr is part of American history.** The reader can tell that this will be an informational piece dealing with a serious subject.

   Finally, your beginning serves to entice the reader deeper into the text. After reading this beginning, the reader will want to know more about this duel.

3. Plan and write a middle that will provide the reader with detailed information and explanation of the opening statement or beginning: *Sample #2 contains several pieces of information about the two men,*

where they lived, why duels were fought, where this duel was fought, the details of this duel, who died, and why Burr was not prosecuted.

4. Plan and write endings that pull the piece together and satisfy the audience so they feel that they have read a meaningful text from the beginning to the end:
Sample #2: This was America's most famous duel, but by no means its last. Slowly individual states outlawed the practice and today dueling with deadly weapons is illegal everywhere in the United States. The first sentence pulls the piece together for the reader. The second sentence gives the reader a more complete understanding of dueling and its demise in American history.

TIPS FOR WRITERS

What Can You Do to Include a Beginning, Middle, and End?

1. Make a simple plan before you write. Include ideas and information for a beginning, middle, and end.

2. In the beginning, introduce your reader to the subject or topic of your writing.

3. In the beginning, set the tone for your piece of writing and try to entice your reader to continue farther into the text.

4. In the middle, write several pieces of detailed information that support your beginning.

5. Design your ending to pull the piece together in a satisfying conclusion.

6. Ask a friend, "Can you identify the sentence(s) that make the beginning of this piece? Do they give you a hint of the topic and voice for the rest of the piece?"

7. Ask a friend, "Please list all of the ideas or information in the middle. Do all of these develop the topic presented in the beginning?"

8. Ask a friend, "Does the ending pull the writing together in a satisfying conclusion?"

Burr vs. Hamilton   1

The famous duel between Alexander Hamilton and Aaron Burr is a part of American history. Burr and Hamilton were politicians and personal enemies. In 1804, Burr challenged Hamilton to a duel. Both men were considered gentlemen and this was thought to be the only honorable way for them to settle their differences. Burr shot Hamilton. He died, but Burr was not prosecuted. Dueling is illegal in the United States today.

Dueling For Honor   2

The famous duel between Alexander Hamilton and Aaron Burr is a part of American history. Burr was the third vice president of the United States from 1801–1805. Hamilton was also a politician and one of our nation's Founding Fathers. Burr and Hamilton were political and personal enemies. At this time, the common man resolved conflicts with fist fights and name-calling. But gentlemen and politicians of the nineteenth century considered their honor to be of the utmost importance. And so, in 1804, when Aaron Burr sent Alexander Hamilton a letter challenging him to a duel, Hamilton felt obliged to defend his honor. Burr and Hamilton met in New Jersey because dueling was illegal in New York, the state in which they both lived. Hamilton made the choice that he would not fire his gun at Burr because he did not wish to kill another man. But Burr had no trouble shooting Hamilton. He died the next day, but Burr could not be prosecuted for he had broken no law. Dueling was accepted as a legitimate means of settling disputes between gentlemen. This was America's most famous duel, but by no means its last. Slowly, individual states outlawed the practice and today dueling with deadly weapons is illegal everywhere in the United States.

Burr Challenges Hamilton 3

Aaron Burr and Alexander Hamilton were both politicians and personal enemies. Gentlemen of the nineteenth century did not settle differences with fist fights. So in 1804, when their conflict grew too great to ignore, Burr sent Hamilton a letter challenging him to a duel. Hamilton felt obliged to defend his honor, and he accepted. They met in New Jersey where dueling was legal. Hamilton made the choice that he would not fire his gun at Burr because he did not wish to kill another man. But Burr did not hesitate to shoot Hamilton in the stomach. He died the next day, but Burr could not be prosecuted for he had broken no law.

Leads

THE QUESTION TO EXPLORE

Do You Want to Read On?

Put your best foot forward. This is sound advice in writing as well as life. A lead, which is the first few words or sentences of a piece of writing, has the power to make a reader sit up and take notice. Well-crafted leads engage readers immediately and entice them to continue on. Leads also help writers introduce content and style to their audience. It's a sneak preview of what's to come. So, it is important to help our students learn how to craft strong leads.

Read many different kinds of leads from picture books, novels, newspaper reports or features, advertisements, and information books. Read one lead and ask:

- Does this lead make you want to read on? Why?
- What do you think the rest of the writing is about?

Literature Links

Leads in picture books tend to be the first few sentences. In a novel, the lead can vary from a few sentences to a few pages. Here are some books that offer students different kinds of leads.

Swamp Angel
by Anne Isaacs

Pink and Say
by Patricia Polacco

Lincoln:
A Photobiography
by Russell Freedman

P.S. Longer Letter Later:
A Novel in Letters
by Paula Danziger
and Ann M. Martin

The Land
by Mildred D. Taylor

Gathering Blue
by Lois Lowry

Counterfeit Son
by Elaine Marie Alphin

Blackwater
by Eve Bunting

Old Yeller
by Fred Gipson

Soldier's Heart
by Gary Paulsen

- Do you hear voice in this lead?
- How would you describe this lead? Is it a dramatic, question, dialogue, reflective, action, contrast, or introductory lead?

Don't always provide students with outstanding leads for this mini-lesson. Help them to recognize the poor or weak lead. This will help your students learn what to avoid in their own writing. I'm always amazed how quickly the students respond after an introduction to leads. They begin to notice different kinds of leads in their own independent reading. Many students enjoy copying some of the strongest leads into their writer's notebook for future reference on style. They become quite critical of their own leads, pushing themselves and their peers to revise those first few words until they do, in fact, pull the reader into the piece. I always tell students that the first purpose of a good lead is to say, "Come here, reader. Look at this. Don't you want more?" If students can accomplish that with their leads, we're off to a great start!

Introducing the Craft Element: Leads

Begin your mini-lesson on leads like this:

Teacher: When a friend calls you with news on the telephone, how much does she need to say before you know if she has good news or bad news?

Students will tell you that they know almost right away. Her voice or what she says gives it away.

Teacher: Suppose your friend has good news to tell you. What might she say?

Students: *Hey, guess what! You won't believe this! Wow, do I have good news for you! Are you ready for some great news?!*

Teacher: What if your friend has some bad news to share with you. What might she say then?

Students: *You might want to sit down for this news. Sorry, but I've got some bad news. This won't make you happy. Hey, I'm sorry that I have to be the one to tell you this.*

Teacher: Is it just the words she says, or do you get a sense of what she might say from HOW she says it?

Students will tell you that they can read her voice, too. They can tell if she is happy or disappointed by the sound of her voice.

Teacher: So, if your friend said, *"You're not going to believe this!"* would you want to hear more? Would you want to know what she was talking about?

Students will all tell you *yes* right away.

Teacher: Are you telling me that in just a few words your friend would be giving you a hint of what she had to say and she would be making you want to hear more?

Students will nod *yes*.

Teacher: That's exactly what a good lead does for our writing. It gives the reader a hint of what's coming up next in the piece. It sets up an expectation for both the topic and the tone or voice. But its most important job is that it compels the reader to continue reading. It's like a lure that attracts the reader to travel deeper into the piece.

Please listen carefully to these two leads:

"Watch out!" I wish I could have heard those words five seconds earlier—before the limb snapped—before I jumped— before the rock crumbled—before I slid thirty feet into the ravine.

I wish someone had warned me sooner. Then maybe I wouldn't have jumped when the limb snapped. And maybe I wouldn't have fallen down the ravine.

Which lead grabbed you more? Which one gave you a greater sample of what the piece will be about and the tone of the voice? Which one made you want to read on?

Most students will tell you that they liked the first lead better. The style and voice of the writing shows frustration. If only the warning had been given earlier, then perhaps this list of unfortunate incidents could have been prevented. They will also share that they want to know what will happen next. Plus, the first lead grabs the reader right away with the words, "Watch out!" The students will also tell you that the second lead doesn't carry the emotion or frustration of the first one—that it seems more distant and removed. Because there is little voice, the reader does not feel as compelled to continue reading.

Teacher: I agree with you. The first lead is more engaging and it does set the stage for the rest of the piece. It introduces us to the character and the immediate situation while "leading" us into the rest of the writing.

Discussing the Craft Element: Leads

Place sample #1 of Set A, B C, D, E, or F (see page 76) of the *Leads* transparencies on the overhead projector. Since we are just working with the first few words of a piece, do not ask questions about focus, development of thorough ideas and information, or vocabulary.

However, now that your students are excited about identifying and using more specific words, don't be surprised if they continue to point out the strong vocabulary. Before you ask questions of the students, give them an opportunity to assess how strong they think the lead is.

> **Teacher:** I will read this lead two times. Please, listen carefully. On a scale of one to ten—ten being the best lead you've ever read in your entire life and one being the most boring, uninviting lead you've ever read—decide what score you would give this example.

After you read the lead, ask four to six students to share their scores. After students announce the scores they've given, ask them why they rated it as they did.

Then ask these questions:

- Does the lead make you want to read on?
- How would you describe this lead? Is it dramatic? Reflective? Introductory? A "grabber"?
- Does it have a question? Dialogue? A contrast? Action?
- Can you tell what this piece might be about?
- Does this lead have voice? Can you describe it?
- Would you be interested in using this kind of lead in your own writing?

Repeat the process outlined above with the other one or two leads in the same set. Of course, answers will vary, but you will see consistency in the leads that students like. Remember, though—students are honest. They will see a need to identify the leads they feel are weak and inadequate. Their scores of 0 to 2 will be one indication. That's great. We want them to recognize poorly written leads. It's just another nudge in the direction of well-crafted writing.

Student reactions to the different leads are likely to include the following:

In Set A, most students will consider #3 to be the strongest lead. They might classify it as a grabber because of the exclamatory statement at the beginning, or they may say it is a contrast because of what Galileo saw and what we can view today. They will surmise that the rest of the piece will be about reflecting telescopes and what distant bodies they help us see. Most students will tell you it has the most voice of the three leads in this set. The voice is both wonder-struck and knowledgable. Students will like the opening and many will begin to use this style in their own writing where appropriate.

In Set B, sample #1 will be the favorite of your students. This lead really makes you want to read on. It could be classified as a dramatic lead combined with a question. The question, of course, is simply the title of the social studies research report, but stating it first helps pull the reader into the piece. The voice is both informal, yet dramatic. The reader would expect to learn what exactly happened in the library and how it changed the speaker's life. Students can write this kind of punchy lead quite successfully. They also enjoy the dramatic effect. Expect to see more of these leads from them soon after this mini-lesson.

Most students prefer sample #1 in Set C. They will identify it as a dialogue lead and mention that the exact conversation between the girls helps create the voice. They might classify the voice as edgy or frightened. Students will share that the rest of the piece will explain what Olivia is doing, why she is frightened, and the outcome of this scene. Intermediate students like to begin narratives with dialogue. Just make sure that you remind them that dialogue needs to push a narrative forward, not bring it to a halt.

Of the two samples in Set D, students generally like #2 better. The vocabulary will be one factor that will separate these two leads. Plus, #2 is more fluent than #1. Students will describe it as an action lead. A lot is happening right away in this opening scene. They will want to read on just to find out what Aunt Luellyn does next. The hint of humor in this scene is another reason to continue reading. Yes, there is a lively, playful voice in this lead. Students will guess that the rest of the piece will be about the confrontation of Aunt Luellyn and the falcon. Many students will be able to craft leads with this *show, don't tell* approach.

Set E offers three average to excellent leads. Your students might have a hearty discussion about which lead is the strongest. Most students will like #3, but many will appreciate #1 as well. Both are introductory leads. The writer whets the reader's appetite with a little information about the who, when, what, and how. Students will know that the rest of the piece will provide more details about the ancient Greeks' pottery making. These leads have an informational voice with a bit of wonder mixed in at the end. Since many students are asked to write in their various content classes, they are likely to experiment with this kind of introductory lead.

In Set F, most students will say that sample #2 is the strongest. They will either describe this as a reflective or poetic lead. In either case, they will recognize the figurative language and relaxed mood that it establishes for the reader. Students might not know for sure if the rest of the writing is about other early morning experiences, or if it will be a contrast showing how a day begins slowly and changes pace as it progresses. Yes, they will say it does have voice. You might hear the words *soft*, *gentle*, *poetic*, or *lyrical* to describe the voice. Not as many students will feel comfortable with this style of writing. Only the more sophisticated writers will experiment with this type of language in some of their leads.

Note: I suggest using only one or two sets of leads in one mini-lesson. Save the others for refresher mini-lessons or as a catapult into revision on leads.

Discussion Points

If students cannot tell you why these samples (#3 in Set A, #1 in Set B, #1 in Set C, #2 in Set D, #3 in Set E, and #2 in Set F) are the strongest leads, put one example on the overhead projector and ask these questions:

- Does this lead provide the topic for the rest of the writing?
- Does this lead make you want to read on? Why?
- Does this lead use specific vocabulary?
- Does this lead have voice? Can you describe it?

Clarify Leads: An Overview of the Craft Element

1. Leads that use specific, active verbs engage readers immediately:
   Like a dive-bomber, the peregrine falcon swooped from the sky and plucked the songbird from the feeder.

2. Dialogue leads develop characters and problems with authentic language:
   Olivia felt tears welling inside her eyes. She silently vowed not to show her fear, not in front of these girls.
   "Are you scared," asked Margaret, as if she already knew the answer.
   "Not at all," answered Olivia, too quickly.
   "Then prove it," said Jeni.

3. Introductory leads offer a taste of the who, what, when, where or how:
   The ancient Greek potters were skilled craftsmen. They created ornate lamps, jars, tiles, vases, and cups with the simplest materials from the earth and a small man-made kiln. Archaeologists today value these pieces of pottery as priceless works of art.

4. Exclamatory leads can set the stage for a piece filled with new or interesting information:
   If Galileo could see us now! Hundreds of thousands of people flock every

year to planetariums around the world to view a universe that he first encountered with the satellites of Jupiter.

5. Strong leads provide a hint of the topic and voice that will be developed in the piece:

   Early morning wraps a person in hope. No worries can penetrate the solitude that the first sunlight spills on the earth. Bathed in sleep, life dreams only of the best.

6. Strong leads pull a reader deeper into the piece:

   How do mountains form? *That was the topic question for my social studies oral report that led me into the Birmingham Public Library. What I learned had nothing to do with mountains, but it certainly changed my life.*

TIPS FOR WRITERS

What Can You Do to Improve Your Leads?

1. Study the different kinds of leads in published writing.
2. Use specific vocabulary in leads.
3. Provide a hint of the topic and voice in the lead.
4. Write two to four different leads and ask a friend, "Which lead pulls you into the writing the most?"

Set A

1 Galileo lived a long time ago before fancy telescopes. But he looked into space and saw the satellites of Jupiter. Today we can see so much more of our universe thanks to the wonderful telescopes in our planetariums.

2 There is so much to see in space. We have powerful reflecting telescopes all over the world. People can go to planetariums and see some of the same things that Galileo saw long ago, plus more.

3 If Galileo could see us now! Hundreds of thousands of people flock every year to planetariums around the world to view a universe that he first encountered with the satellites of Jupiter. Today, powerful reflecting telescopes help us examine celestial bodies that are millions of miles away.

Set B

1 *How do mountains form?* That was the topic question for my social studies oral report that led me into the Birmingham Public Library. What I learned had nothing to do with mountains, but it certainly changed my life.

2 I went to the library to research how mountains are made for my social studies class. I learned a lot, but it had nothing to do with mountains.

Set C

1 Olivia felt tears welling inside her eyes. She silently vowed not to show her fear, not in front of these girls.

"Are you scared," asked Margaret, as if she already knew the answer.

"Not at all," answered Olivia, too quickly.

"Then prove it," said Jeni.

Olivia's hand shook as she reached out and pushed the door open.

2 Olivia was scared that she might cry. But she didn't want to, not in front of these girls.

They asked her if she were afraid. But she said no.

They told her to prove it.

So Olivia reached out and pushed the door open.

Set D

1 Like a dive-bomber, the falcon dropped out of the sky and grabbed the songbird from the feeder. Inside, Aunt Luellyn watched in horror. So she grabbed her broom, went outside, and swung it at the falcon.

2 Like a dive-bomber, the peregrine falcon swooped from the sky and plucked the songbird from the feeder. Appalled, Aunt Luellyn dropped the saucer she was washing and ran outside, swinging her broom over her head with the force of a hurricane.

Set E

1 Ancient Greek potters worked hard. With materials from the earth and a kiln, they were able to create lamps, jars, tiles, vases, and cups that archaeologists today consider priceless.

2 Long ago, Greek men made wonderful pottery. With a few simple materials they molded fancy lamps, jars, tiles, vases, and cups. People today think these artifacts are beautiful.

3 The ancient Greek potters were skilled craftsmen. They created ornate lamps, jars, tiles, vases, and cups with the simplest materials from the earth and a small man-made kiln. Archaeologists today value these pieces of pottery as priceless works of art.

Set F

1. Early morning is great. It's so quiet and peaceful. Every living thing stretches in the first sunlight and dreams about what it can do.

2. Early morning wraps a person in hope. No worries can penetrate the solitude that the first sunlight spills on the earth. Bathed in sleep, life dreams only of the best.

3. Early morning is so hopeful. I never worry about things when I see the sun rise. I just think ahead to all of the possibilities.

Bibliography

Alexander, Lloyd. *The Fortune-Tellers*. New York: Dutton Children's Books, 1992.

Alphin, Elaine Marie. *Counterfeit Son*. San Diego: Harcourt, 2000.

Bauer, Joan. *Hope Was Here*. New York: Putnam, 2000.

Bradby, Marie. *More Than Anything Else*. New York: Orchard, 1995.

Bunting, Eve. *Blackwater*. New York: HarperCollins, 1999.

Danziger, Paula and Ann M. Martin. *P.S. Longer Letter Later: A Novel in Letters*. New York: Scholastic, 1998.

DiCamillo, Kate. *Because of Winn-Dixie*. New York: Candlewick, 2000.

Freedman, Russell. *Lincoln: A Photobiography*. New York: Clarion, 1987.

Gipson, Fred. *Old Yeller*. New York: Harper & Row, 1956.

Haddix, Margaret Peterson. *Among The Hidden*. New York: Simon & Schuster, 1998.

Hesse, Karen. *Out of the Dust*. New York: Scholastic, 1997.

Isaacs, Anne. *Swamp Angel*. New York: Dutton Children's Books, 1994.

Lowry, Lois. *Gathering Blue*. Boston: Houghton Mifflin, 2000.

MacLachlan, Patricia. *Baby*. New York: Delacorte, 1993.

Martin, Jacqueline Briggs. *Snowflake Bentley*. Boston: Houghton Mifflin, 1998.

Paulsen, Gary. *The Rifle*. San Diego: Harcourt, 1995.

Paulsen, Gary. *Soldier's Heart*. New York: Scholastic, 1998.

Polacco, Patricia. *Pink and Say*. New York: Philomel, 1994.

Rylant, Cynthia. *The Van Gogh Cafe*. San Diego: Harcourt, 1995.

Taylor, Mildred D. *The Land*. New York: Penguin Putnam, 2001.

Wattenberg, Jane. *Henny-Penny*. New York: Scholastic, 2000.

Wiles, Deborah. *Freedom Summer*. New York: Atheneum Books for Young Readers, 2001.

Yolen, Jane. *Owl Moon*. New York: Philomel, 1987.